Indian Fusion Cooking

Shobhna Sahgal

Ocean Books Pvt. Ltd.

ISO 9001:2000 Publishers

Published by
Ocean Books (P) Ltd.
4/19 Asaf Ali Road,
New Delhi-110 002 (INDIA)

ISBN 81-88322-89-X
Indian Fusion Cooking

Edition
First, 2006

Price
Rs. 250.00 (Rs. Two hundred fifty only)

Printed at
Graphic World, New Delhi

Introduction

In this recipe book, I have tried to include recipes for all types of meals, from family snacks to entertainment meals, for both vegetarians and non-vegetarians.

Several western dishes have been blended with Indian spices to make them more suitable for the Indian palate. All the recipes are simple and easy to prepare, keeping the beginner cook in mind. In fact, this book came about when my three children, all of whom have moved abroad, kept asking me for recipes that they could prepare, using ingredients that were easily available in the UK and US.

I hope this book will really add pleasure to your day-to-day cooking, while helping you prepare more exciting meals for special occasions.

—Shobhna Sahgal

Cook-book Notes

KEY INDIAN SPICES

Listed below are some spices and ingredients that are commonly used in Indian cooking and have been used in several of the recipes in this cook-book:

- Coriander powder (dhaniya)
- Cumin powder (jeera)
- Chilli powder
- Mango powder (amchoor)
- Turmeric (haldi)
- Cinnamon (dalchini)
- Cardamom (elaichi)
- Chat Masala (mixed spices)
- Tandoori powder
- garam masala (mixed spices)

Indian recipes also use plenty of:

- onions
- garlic
- ginger
- tomatoes
- coriander leaves

...so before you start cooking, make sure you stock up your larder with these key ingredients!

Translation of Indian Ingredients

Adrak	Ginger
Ajwain	Thyme
Akhrot	Walnut
Amchoor	Mango powder
Badam	Almond
Besan	Gram flour
Dalchini	Cinnamon
Dhania	Coriander
Elaichi	Cardamom
Garam masala	Mixed spices
Ghee	Clarified butter
Haldi	Turmeric
Imli	Tamarind
Jeera	Cumin seed
Kaju	Cashewnut
Kala namak	Black salt
Kali mirch	Black pepper
Keema	Minced lamb
Kesar	Saffron
Khaskhas	Poppy seed
Kishmish	Raisin
Lahsun	Garlic
Lavang	Cloves
Methi	Fenugreek seed
Moongphali	Groundnut
Narial	Coconut
Paneer	Cottage cheese
Pista	Pistachio
Pudhina	Mint
Rai	Mustard seed
Saunf	Aniseeds
Shahjeera	Caraway seed
Tej pattha	Bay leaf
Til	Sesame seed
Tulsi	Basil

Oven Temperature Chart

The table below is an approximate guide to oven temperatures as indicated in the recipes in this book. Oven temperatures vary greatly and it is best to refer to the manufacturer's guide for greater accuracy.

Oven	Electric (Fahrenheit)	Electric (Celsius)	Gas
Very Cool	225-250	110-130	½
Cool	250-300	140-150	1, 2
Moderate	325-350	160-180	3, 4
Moderately hot	375-400	190-200	5, 6
Hot	425-450	220-230	7, 8
Very Hot	475-500	240-260	9

Glossary of Cooking Terms

Bake — Cook in an oven in dry heat

Batter — A mixture of dry and liquid ingredients beaten together

Beat — Stir briskly

Blanch — Immerse in boiling water. Usually to remove the skin of nuts.

Blend — To mix ingredients thoroughly preferably using an electric blender

Chop — To cut into small pieces

Cream — To mix thoroughly until mixture is smooth

Dice — To cut into small even-sized pieces

Dissolve — To mix a dry substance into water

Dot — To scatter a small amount of the ingredient over the surface of the food

Dough — A mixture of flour and a liquid kneaded until it is smooth

Dredge — To coat the food with some ingredients

Dust — To sprinkle lightly

Flake — To separate the food lightly into small pieces, particularly boiled fish or chicken

Fold — To gently stir an additional ingredient into a mixture

Garnish — To decorate the outside of a food with an additional ingredient to make it look more attractive

Grate — To shred something by rubbing it against a grater

Grill — To cook under direct heat

Grind — To crush ingredients into a powder or paste

Icing — To cover the top of a food with a sugar-based coating

Knead — To work the dough with both hands

Marinate — To soak food in a liquid mixture

Mash — To crush any soft substance

Mince — To cut into very tiny pieces

Mix — To combine the ingredients by stirring

Paste — Soft, thick and slightly moist mixture produced by grinding

Pit — To remove the seeds from a fruit

Puree — A smooth thick mixture obtained by straining the ingredients

Pre-heat — To warm the oven to a stated temperature before placing the food in it

Saute	—	To fry the ingredient in a small amount of oil or butter until it is tender
Scoop	—	To remove the inner pulp of a fruit or vegetable
Sift	—	To pass the ingredient through a fine sieve
Simmer	—	To boil on low heat
Soak	—	To immerse in a liquid
Steam	—	To cook over a pan of boiling water; or in a steamer
Stew	—	To cook slowly in a little liquid inside a covered pan
Stock	—	The water in which vegetables or meat pieces have been boiled for a long while
Strain	—	To remove solid parts from a liquid mixture
Whip	—	To stir briskly until the mixture is thickened
Whisk	—	To stir briskly until an ingredient (usually eggs) is light and fluffy

Table of Contents

Snacks & Starters

PRAWN IN FISH ROLLS

A divine snack that never fails to please. I usually use the Indian Bekti fish for this recipe, but Cod or Plaice taste just as good.

Preparation time:
20 minutes

Serving size:
6 - 8 rolls

250 gms white fish cut into thin, flat slices for rolls

FILLING

½ cup prawns, cleaned and chopped

1 onion chopped

2 tbsp green chillies chopped

1 tsp Soya sauce

1 tsp garlic crushed

Salt to taste

COATING

4 tbsp flour seasoned with salt and pepper

1 egg beaten with

2 tsp water

1 cup fine bread crumbs

Oil for frying

1. Heat the oil in a frying pan and fry the onions and chillies.
2. Add the prawns, then the garlic, Soya sauce and salt. Cook until dry.
3. Place the fish slices on a chopping board. Spoon 1 tsp of the prawn mixture in the middle of each fish slice. Roll the fish slices.
4. Carefully coat each fish roll in the prepared flour. Then dip it in the egg and roll it in the breadcrumbs, taking care to seal it completely.
5. Deep-fry the fish to a golden brown.

Serve hot with Yogurt Dip or Chilli Sauce (see under *Chutneys, Dips and Sauces*).

CRUNCHY CHEESE TOAST

This variation of the cheese toast makes a great snack for children and grown ups alike.

Preparation time:
20 minutes

Serving size:
6 portions

½ cup grated Cheddar cheese

¼ cup mayonnaise

1 onion finely chopped

2 tbsp chopped coriander leaves

2 tbsp roasted peanuts (crushed)

6 slices of bread

1. Combine all the ingredients in a bowl and mix well.
2. Spread the mixture evenly on the bread slices.
3. Arrange the bread on a greased baking tray and grill for about 10 minutes, or until the cheese mixture starts to bubble.
4. Serve hot with Sweet Lemon Pickle (Pg 39).

MASALA PANEER

This makes a great Indian snack that is suitable for vegetarians.

Preparation time:
20 minutes plus
1 hour marinating

Serving size:
15-20 pieces

250 gm paneer cubes
1 tsp lime juice
1 tsp coriander powder
½ tsp cumin powder
1 tsp chilli powder (optional)
2 tsp garlic paste
1 tsp ginger paste
3 tbsp vinegar
2 tbsp gram flour
1 tsp salt
1 tbsp Chat Masala (optional as garnish)

1. Mix all the ingredients in a bowl to form a thick paste.
2. Marinate the paneer cubes in the paste for about 1 hour.
3. Deep fry the paneer cubes until golden brown.
4. Sprinkle some Chat Masala over the paneer.

Serve with salad greens.

CRISPY BEER PAKORAS

These delicious snacks are easy to cook and are great for cocktails parties.

Preparation time:
10 minutes

Cooking time:
10 minutes

Serving size:
20-25 pieces

1 cucumber
2 boiled potatoes
1 small aubergine
Oil for frying

BATTER
1 cup flour
2 tbsp rice flour
1 cup beer
1 tsp red chilli powder
1 tsp salt

1. Combine all the ingredients for the batter in a bowl and mix until it is smooth and thick.
2. Chop all the vegetables into 2 inch long sticks.
3. Heat the oil in a wok or frying pan. Dip the vegetables in the batter and deep fry until crispy.

Serve with Garlic Mayonnaise or Chilli Sauce (see under *Chutneys, Dips and Sauces*).

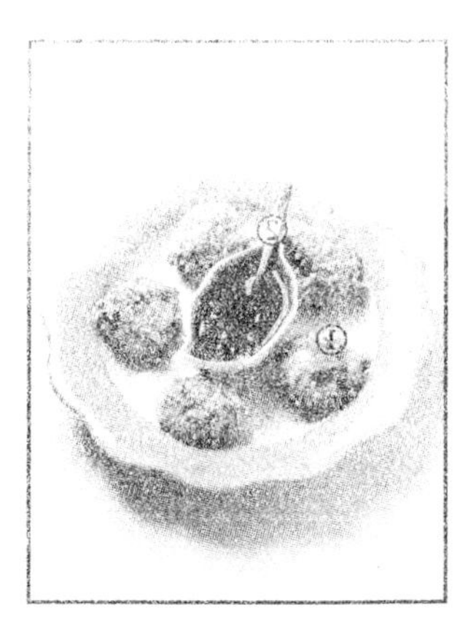

CHILLED PANEER BALLS

These delicious cottage cheese balls require no cooking!

Preparation time:
20 minutes plus
1 hour chilling time

Serving size:
15-20 pieces

½ cup grated paneer
4 tbsp mayonnaise
1 cucumber chopped
1 capsicum chopped
½ cup chopped spring onions
2 tbsp chopped coriander leaves
½ cup chopped roasted peanuts
1 tsp salt
1 tsp pepper

1. Add the cottage cheese and mayonnaise into a bowl and mix well until the mixture is smooth.
2. Stir in all the remaining ingredients (except the peanuts).
3. Cover the bowl and chill the mixture in the refrigerator for about 1 hour.
4. Remove the bowl from the refrigerator. Roll the mixture into small balls.
5. Crush the peanuts on a flat surface with a rolling pin. Roll the balls in the crushed peanuts.
6. Arrange the balls on a serving dish. Serve with Tomato Dip (Pg. 52).

① Chilled Paneer Balls
② Tomato Dip—p. 52

FRIED BANANAS

Fried raw bananas make a delicious snack, and are very popular in many parts of Africa and South Asia.

Preparation time:
20 minutes

Serving size:
8 portions

4 large raw bananas boiled
1 tsp garlic paste
1 tsp ginger paste
1 tsp green chilli paste
1 tsp ground ajwain (thyme)
2 tbsp plain yogurt
1 tbsp cornflour
1 tsp salt
Bread crumbs
Oil for frying

1. Slice the bananas lengthwise into 4 inch long pieces.
2. Mix all the ingredients to form a batter and spread it over the sliced bananas.
3. Cover the coated banana slices with breadcrumbs and deep fry until they turn golden brown.

Serve with Mustard Sauce on a bed of salad.

① Fried Bananas
② Mustard Sauce—p. 47

TANGY FISH TIKKA

These make a tasty starter and go well with Indian as well as European main courses.

Preparation time:
10 minutes plus
3-4 hours marinating time

Cooking time:
10 minutes

Serving size:
8-10 pieces

500 gm boneless fish cut into 2 inch cubes

Oil for frying

1 onion (optional)

1 tbsp Chat Masala (optional as garnish)

MARINADE

2 tbsp lime juice

1 tbsp vinegar

2 tsp coriander powder

1 tsp chilli powder

2 tsp garlic paste

2 tsp ginger paste

2 tsp mango powder

2 tbsp cornflour

1 tsp salt

Pinch of red Tandoori colour

1. Place the fish in a flat dish. Mix all the ingredients for the marinade in a small bowl and pour over the fish. Marinate the fish for about 3-4 hours in the refrigerator.
2. Heat the oil in a frying pan. Carefully deep fry the fish for about 4-5 minutes.
3. Serve hot.

Serve with fine onion rings and sprinkle some Chat Masala over the fish for added flavour.

CHILLED AUBERGINE (BRINJAL)

Preparation/Cooking time:
20 minutes

Serving size:
4 portions

2 medium-sized aubergines
1½ cups yogurt
2 tsp garlic paste
2 green chillies very finely chopped (optional)
1 tsp salt
Oil for frying

1. Slice the aubergines into thin rings.
2. Heat the oil in a frying pan and fry the aubergine slices until they turn golden brown.
3. Drain the oil and arrange the aubergines on a glass platter.
4. Mix the garlic paste and yogurt in a bowl. Add the green chillies (optional) and the salt to the yogurt mixture.
5. Pour the yogurt mixture over the aubergine slices.
6. Refrigerate for at least 1 hour and serve chilled.

OPEN SANDWICHES

These may be served warm or chilled.

Preparation time:
30 minutes

Serving size:
4 portions

4 bread rolls sliced into two

1 tbsp butter

2 tbsp Mint Chutney (Pg 42)

2 tbsp White Sauce (Pg 40)

½ cup mayonnaise, 4 tbsp boiled corn

2 tbsp carrots, boiled and chopped

2 tbsp roasted peanuts

1 slice pineapple, chopped

2 green chillies, chopped

2 tbsp chopped onions

1 tbsp chopped coriander

Salt and Pepper

1. Butter the slices of bread. Then spread some Mint Chutney over the slices and place them on a flat baking dish.
2. In a bowl mix together all the remaining ingredients, adjusting the salt and pepper according to your taste.
3. Spread the mixture evenly on the bread slices.
4. Bake the slices in a pre-heated moderate oven for 10 minutes. Then place them under the grill for a couple of minutes to brown the top lightly.

SPICY BREAD ROLLS

These soft bread rolls have a unique flavour and fragrance, and are best when served warm.

Preparation time:	**Cooking time:**	**Serving size:**
30 minutes plus 2 hours	20 minutes	15-20 rolls

4 cups flour
¼ cup butter
½ tsp cumin seeds
½ tsp red chilli powder
2 tsp dry yeast
2 tsp sugar
1 tsp salt
1 cup milk
¼ cup lukewarm water

1. Melt the butter in a saucepan. Add the milk, sugar and salt and stir well.
2. Pour the warm water into a large mixing bowl and dissolve the yeast in it.
3. Slowly add the milk mixture from the saucepan into the bowl.
4. Add the remaining ingredients into the bowl and knead well until the dough is smooth.
5. Cover the dough and keep it in a warm place until it doubles in size. (About 2 hours).
6. Divide the dough into 15-20 balls and twist into rolls.
7. Arrange the rolls on a baking tray, cover and set aside for about 30 minutes.
8. Bake in a pre-heated oven at 400^0 F for about 20 minutes or until the crust turns light brown.

MERINGUE CHICKS

These make an adorable snack for a children's party.

Preparation time: 20 minutes

Baking time: 3-4 hours

Serving size: 15-20 chicks

2 egg whites

125 gm sugar (ground to a fine powder)

Food colouring (optional)

1. Grease a baking tray with a little butter and dust over with some flour.
2. Beat the egg whites and sugar until the mixture is stiff and dry.
3. Fill the mixture in a piping bag with a plain big nozzle.
4. On the baking tray, carefully pipe 2 inch oval shapes that are slightly pointed at one end, and rounded on the other side, to look like a chick with a head and tail.
5. Place in a pre-heated hot oven, and immediately reduce the oven temperature to a minimum. Leave the chicks to bake for 3-4 hours.

Blue, yellow, red and cocoa colours may be added to create different coloured chicks.

EGGLESS FRUIT CAKE

This cake is so light and fluffy, your guests won't believe that it is made without eggs.

Preparation time:
15 minutes

Baking time:
35-40 minutes

Serving size:
Serves 4

1 cup flour
1 ½ tsp baking powder
½ tsp baking soda
¼ cup butter
½ cup ground sugar
½ cup currants
¼ cup dried mixed fruit
1 tsp vanilla essence
¼ cup milk
8 inch round baking dish

1. In a large bowl, add the butter and sugar and beat well together using an electric beater.
2. Add the milk, dried fruits, currants and vanilla essence.
3. Fold in the flour, baking soda and baking powder and beat the mixture together with a wooden spoon.
4. Grease the baking dish with some butter and pour the batter carefully into the dish.
5. Bake in a pre-heated moderate oven for about 35-40 minutes.

Let the cake cool down to room temperature before serving.

JAM-FILLED COOKIES

Preparation/
Cooking time:
30 minutes

Serving size:
20 cookies

3 cups flour
1 tsp baking powder
1 tsp vanilla essence
1 cup powdered sugar
100 gm butter
1 egg
2 tsp gelatine
2 tbsp cornflour
2 tbsp water
Strawberry jam
Flower-shaped cookie cutter

1. Beat the butter and sugar together in a bowl until the mixture is light and fluffy. Add the egg and vanilla essence.
2. Sieve the flour and baking powder together and add to the bowl. Mix well and chill the dough for 1 hour.
3. Using a rolling pin, roll the chilled dough on a lightly floured surface to about ⅛ inch thickness.
4. Cut out about 40 flower-shapes. For half the shapes, cut out a small round in the centre. Place all the shapes in a baking tray.
5. Bake the cookies in a pre-heated moderate oven for 10-12 minutes. Remove the cookies from the oven and leave them to cool.
6. Mix the cornflour with water. Heat the jam in a pan. Add the cornflour and gelatine and simmer for 2 minutes. Remove and set aside to cool.
7. Once cooled, place 1 tsp of jam on each of the flower-shaped cookies, and place the cookies with the holes in them on top.
8. Arrange the cookies on a platter and sprinkle some powdered sugar over them before serving.

QUICK MACAROONS

A great snack for the last-minute guest.

Preparation time:
15 minutes

Baking time:
10-12 minutes

Serving size:
25 macaroons

1 cup condensed milk
2 cups desiccated coconut
1 tsp vanilla essence
2 tbsp chopped almonds
2 tbsp raisins

1. Combine all the ingredients in a bowl and mix well.
2. On a greased baking tray, place one-teaspoon size portions of the mixture about 1 inch apart.
3. Bake in a pre-heated moderate oven for about 10-12 minutes or until lightly browned.
4. Remove from the tray while still warm and arrange on a serving dish to cool.

CHOCOLATE PINWHEELS

These cookies are simple to bake and make a tasty snack for children.

Preparation time:	**Chilling time:**	**Serving size:**
20 minutes	1 hour	15-20 cookies

100 gm butter
100 gm sugar
200 gm flour
1 egg
1 tsp vanilla essence
3 tbsp cocoa powder

1. In a large bowl, cream together the butter and sugar. Beat the egg separately and add it to the butter and sugar mixture.
2. Add the flour and mix thoroughly until the dough is firm. Divide the dough into 2 portions. Place half the dough in a separate bowl and stir in the cocoa powder to make brown coloured dough.
3. Roll the plain dough into a rectangular shape about $^{1}/_{8}$ inch thick. Then, separately roll out the brown dough into a rectangle of the same size.
4. Carefully lay the brown dough on top of the plain dough and roll up both together from the long edge to form a cylinder. Wrap the dough cylinder in cling film and chill in the freezer for about 1 hour.
5. Once chilled, remove the dough from the freezer and, using a sharp knife, slice it into thin round slices (about ¼ inch thick) to form pinwheel shapes.
6. Bake the chocolate pinwheels in a preheated moderate oven for about 12-15 minutes. Leave to cool.
7. Arrange the cookies on a platter, and dust lightly with powdered sugar before serving.

LOLLY BISCUITS

A colourful and tasty treat that is a big hit at any children's party.

Preparation time: 30 minutes

Chilling time: 15 minutes

Serving size: 15 biscuits

FOR THE DOUGH

100 gm butter

100 gm sugar

200 gm flour

1 egg beaten

1 tsp vanilla essence

FOR THE BISCUITS

15 ice cream sticks

Assorted cookie cutter shapes

FOR THE ICING

1 cup sifted icing sugar

2 tbsp boiling water

Food colouring

MAKING THE DOUGH

1. Cream the butter and sugar together in a bowl.
2. Add the beaten egg and vanilla essence.
3. Stir in the flour and mix well to form a firm dough.

TO MAKE THE LOLLY BISCUITS

1. Roll the dough to about 1/8 inch thick sheet and cut out different shapes (rounds, stars, animal shapes etc.) making sure that there are 2 of each kind.
2. Butter the inside of a baking tray and lightly dust some flour over it.
3. Place half the shapes in the tray and brush over them with some water or egg white. Place an ice cream stick in the centre of each shape and place the matching shape over it.
4. Bake in a preheated oven for about 15 minutes.
5. Remove the lolly biscuits from the oven and allow them to cool down before decorating

them with icing.

6. Put the icing sugar in a bowl and add the water. Stir continuously, until thick and smooth.
7. Use one half of the icing to completely cover one side of the lolly biscuits.
8. Divide the other half of the icing into small portions and mix different food colouring in each portion. Use different coloured icing to decorate the lolly biscuits, making eyes, noses, lips, cheeks and hair.

① Lolly Biscuits
② Jam-Filled Cookies—p. 26
③ Chocolate Eclairs—p. 135

SHAMMI KEBABS

Cooking time:
45 minutes

Serving size:
8 portions

500 gms minced lamb meat
2 onions cut into halves
1 pod garlic
1 inch long ginger
4 black cardamoms
2 green cardamoms
4 cloves
20 whole black peppers
1 inch long cinnamon stick
½ cup chana dal (Split Gram)
1 tsp chilli powder
1 cup water
1 egg
salt
Oil for frying

For the stuffing

1 onion chopped
2 tbsp chopped coriander
1 tbsp chopped mint leaves
2 green chillies (optional)

For the garnish

1 onion cut into rings
1 tomato cut into thin slices

1. Put all the ingredients (except the egg) in a deep cooking pan. Cover with the lid and cook till the meat is dry (no water is remaining).
2. Let the mixture cool down and then grind into a fine paste.
3. Add the egg and salt and mix well.
4. Make about 15–20 equal size balls with the mixture.
5. Stuff each ball with the chopped onions, chillies, coriander and mint leaves.
6. Flatten the balls and deep fry them.
7. Serve with onion rings, tomato slices and Yogurt Dip (Pg. 50).

① Shammi Kebabs
② Yogurt Dip—p. 50

CAULIFLOWER PAKORAS

These pakoras are so irresistible that you should always make more than you think you will need—they disappear very quickly.

Preparation time:
30 minutes

Cooking time:
20 minutes

Serving size:
6-8 portions

1 medium sized cauliflower
¼ cup plain flour
¼ cup rice flour
¼ cup gram flour (Besan)
2 tbsp tomato ketchup
1 tsp chilli powder
4 tbsp onion paste
1 tbsp garlic paste
1 tsp garam masala
Salt to taste
Oil for frying

1. Break the cauliflower into florets.
2. Mix together the onion paste, garlic paste, garam masala and salt. Smear this mixture onto the cauliflower florets and set aside for about 30 minutes.
3. In a large bowl, mix together the plain flour, rice flour and gram flour. Add the tomato ketchup, chilli powder, salt and water to make a thick batter.
4. Heat the oil in a frying pan.
5. Dip the seasoned cauliflower florets in the batter and deep fry till they are crisp and golden brown.
6. Serve hot with Tomato Dip (Pg. 52).

CRUNCHY WALNUT CHICKEN

These nutty chicken morsels are delicious and may be served with a tangy and spicy sauce.

Cooking time:
20 minutes

Serving size:
12–15 pieces

500 gms boneless chicken breasts
2 egg whites
4 tsp cornflour
2 tbsp sherry
½ cup chopped walnuts
Salt and pepper
1 cup oil for frying

1. Cut the chicken breast into bite size pieces.
2. Mix together the salt, pepper and sherry. Add the chicken pieces into this mixture.
3. In a separate bowl, beat the egg whites lightly. Add the corn flour and mix well.
4. Heat the oil in a frying pan.
5. Dip the chicken pieces into the egg and cornflour mixture. Then coat each piece with the chopped walnuts and deep fry the chicken pieces until they turn light brown.
6. Drain the chicken on a paper towel. Serve hot with Mint Chutney (Pg. 42).

MASALA CAKE

This makes a delicious and nutritious savoury snack.

Preparation/ Cooking time:
1 hour

Serving Size:
4-6 portions

1 cup flour

2 tsp baking powder

1 tsp salt

½ tsp cumin seeds

½ cup butter

2 tsp sugar

2 eggs

1 onion chopped

1 green chilli chopped

1 piece of ginger chopped

½ cup shelled peas

½ capsicum chopped

About ¼ cup milk

For the garnish
Tomato ketchup

2 tbsp grated coconut or grated carrots

1. Sieve the flour, baking powder and salt together in a bowl, then add the cumin seeds.
2. Beat the eggs separately.
3. In a separate bowl, beat the butter and sugar together till light and fluffy.
4. Add the beaten eggs and the flour mixture to the creamed butter, one spoonful at a time. Continue beating the mixture, while alternately adding the flour and the beaten eggs.
5. Fold in all the remaining ingredients.
6. Slowly add in milk to get a mixture with a smooth consistency.
7. Pour the mixture on to a greased baking tin and bake in a preheated moderate hot oven for 30–35 minutes.
8. Remove the cake from the oven and let it cool down.
9. Apply some tomato ketchup on top of the cake and garnish with grated coconut or grated carrots. Serve with Mint Chutney (Pg. 42).

Pickles, Dips & Sauces

GRATED MANGO PICKLE

Mango pickles may be enjoyed with all Indian dishes.

Preparation/ Cooking time:
20 minutes

Serving size:
Makes one medium sized jar of pickle

- 2 green mangoes peeled and grated
- 1 tsp mustard seeds
- 1 tsp fenugreek seeds
- ½ tsp turmeric powder
- 3 tbsp chilli powder
- 2 tbsp salt
- 4 tbsp sugar
- 3 tbsp oil

1. Heat the oil in a saucepan. Add the mustard seeds and fenugreek seeds and fry for about 2-3 minutes.
2. Add the grated mangoes and turmeric powder mixing well for a further 2-3 minutes.
3. Cover the pan and cook on low heat for about 10 minutes.
4. Add the salt, sugar and chilli powder. Mix well and cook uncovered for about 5 more minutes.
5. Turn off the heat and let the mixture cool down for about 1 hour.
6. Store in a glass jar.

SWEET LEMON PICKLE

Another very popular pickle in India is the sweet Lemon Pickle which is enjoyed with snacks and main dishes.

Preparation time:
2 days

Cooking time:
15 minutes
Plus 5-6 days storage time

Serving size:
Makes one medium-sized jar of pickle

5 lemons
¼ cup sugar
2 tsp red chilli powder
2 tsp thinly sliced ginger
2 tsp salt

1. Soak the lemons in salty water and refrigerate the mixture for two days.
2. Remove the lemons from the water and dry well with a paper towel.
3. Cut each lemon into 8 pieces and remove the seeds.
4. Mix all the remaining ingredients in a bowl. Add the lemon pieces to the mixture.
5. Store the mixture in a glass jar and keep it out in the sun.
6. The pickle will be ready to eat in 5/6 days.

BASIC WHITE SAUCE

This sauce forms the basis of many European dishes. Here a little bit of lime juice is added to give it that extra special flavour.

Preparation time:
10 minutes

Serving size:
Makes 1 cup of sauce

25 gm butter
25 gm flour
1 cup milk
½ tsp lime juice
1 tsp salt
¼ tsp pepper

1. Melt the butter in a small saucepan over medium heat. Stir in the flour and allow it to brown a little.
2. Pour in the milk, stirring vigorously, until it forms a smooth paste.
3. Remove from the stove top and add the salt, pepper and lime juice.

EGGLESS MAYONNAISE

Preparation time:
20 minutes plus

Serving size:
Makes about 1 bowl of mayonnaise

6 tbsp powder milk
½ cup oil
1 tsp mustard powder
1 tsp sugar
2 tsp vinegar
1 tsp lemon juice
½ cup whipped cream
1 tsp salt
¼ tsp pepper

1. Add the sugar, mustard, salt and pepper in a bowl.
2. Add the powder milk and mix well.
3. Add the oil, one drop at a time, stirring continuously.
4. Add the vinegar and the lime juice and mix well.
5. Fold in the cream.

MINT CHUTNEY

Mint Chutney is one of the most popular Indian sauces and may be served as an accompaniment with any appetiser.

Preparation time:
10 minutes

Serving size:
1 small bowl of chutney

1 bunch mint leaves

1 bunch coriander leaves

6 garlic cloves

1 inch long ginger

2 tsp lemon juice or tamarind juice

1 tbsp cold water

1 tsp salt

½ tsp sugar

4 green chillies (optional)

1. Grind all the ingredients together with the cold water to form a smooth paste.
2. Adjust the salt and chillies according to your taste.

Store in an airtight glass jar in the refrigerator.

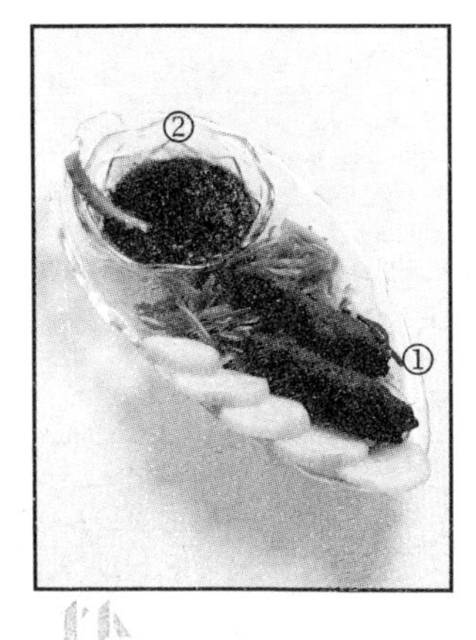

① Vegetable Seekh Kebabs—p. 72
② Mint Chutney

SPICY DATE CHUTNEY

This chutney may be used both as a dip or as a topping over many main dishes.

Preparation/ Cooking time:
15 minutes

Serving size:
Makes 1 bowl of chutney

100 gm dates
50 gm tamarind soaked in water
2 tbsp sugar
1 tsp black salt
1 tsp chilli powder
½ tsp cumin seed powder
1 cup water

1. Squeeze out the juice from the soaked tamarind.
2. Grind the dates into a smooth paste.
3. Combine all the remaining ingredients in a bowl. Add the tamarind juice and date paste and mix well.
4. Pour the mixture into a saucepan and cook on high heat for 5 minutes.
5. Cool for about an hour and use it as topping or with snacks.

The chutney may be stored in a glass jar and refrigerated for up to 1 month.

① Fish Punjabi—p. 89
② Spicy Date Chutney

GARLIC MAYONNAISE

Garlic Mayonnaise is wonderful as a dip or as a topping sauce for meat dishes.

Preparation time:
20 minutes

Serving size:
1 small bowl of mayonnaise

2 eggs
1½ tsp garlic paste
1 cup oil
1 tsp salt
1 tsp sugar
1 tsp pepper
1 tsp vinegar
2 tbsp lemon juice
2 tbsp beer

1. Add the eggs, salt, pepper, garlic paste and 4 tbsp oil in a blender and mix until smooth.
2. Open the blender and slowly add the remaining oil, lemon juice and vinegar – one drop at a time.
3. Continue to blend the mixture until the mayonnaise is thick.
4. Transfer the mayonnaise into a bowl and stir in the beer.

MUSTARD SAUCE

This mildly spicy sauce makes a wonderful accompaniment for many fish dishes.

Preparation time:
15 minutes

Serving size:
1 cup of sauce

½ cup double cream
1 tsp mustard seeds
1 tsp freshly ground pepper
1 tsp salt
1 tbsp cold water

1. Grind the mustard seeds with the water to make a smooth paste.
2. Pour the double cream into a bowl. Add the mustard seed paste and mix well.
3. Add the salt and pepper.

SPICY AUBERGINE (BRINJAL) SAUCE

Preparation/Cooking time:
15 minutes

Serving size:
1 bowl of sauce

2 aubergines
2 spring onions chopped
2 green chillies chopped
1 tsp finely chopped ginger
1 tsp garlic paste
2 tbsp vinegar
1 tbsp tamarind pulp strained
1 tsp salt

1. Cook the aubergines in salty boiling water until they are soft. Drain the excess water and skin the aubergines.
2. Using a fork, mash the skinned aubergines in a bowl.
3. Add all the remaining ingredients and mix well.
4. Chill and serve cold.

CHILLI SAUCE

This is a traditional Chilli Sauce that may be stored in glass jars and refrigerated for up to 4 months.

Preparation/Cooking time:
1 hour soaking 15 minutes

Serving size:
1 bowl of sauce

100 gm large red chillies

4 tbsp vinegar

Salt according to taste

1. Soak the chillies in vinegar for about an hour.
2. Place the entire mixture of chillies and vinegar in a blender and grind into a thick paste.
3. Add the salt and store in a glass jar.

YOGURT DIP

This dish is referred to as 'Raita' in India and is served as an accompaniment with vegetables and meat dishes.

Preparation/Cooking time:
15 minutes

Serving size:
Makes 1 bowl

100 gm plain yogurt

2 tsp cold water

1 small onion, finely chopped

2 tbsp chopped coriander

1 tbsp chopped mint

2 green chillies chopped (optional)

½ tsp salt

1. Beat the yogurt with the water until smooth and thick.
2. Add the remaining ingredients and mix together.
3. Pour into a glass bowl and serve chilled.

COCONUT CHUTNEY

Preparation/Cooking time:
15 minutes

Serving size:
Makes 1 bowl of chutney

½ coconut grated
2 tbsp chopped coriander
1 tbsp ground ginger
2 green chillies, finely chopped
2 tbsp warm water
¼ tsp salt
½ tsp mustard seeds
1 tbsp oil

1. Add the grated coconut, chopped coriander, warm water, ground ginger, chillies and salt in a bowl and mix well together.
2. Heat the oil in a frying pan. Add the mustard seeds until they being to pop. Immediately, pour the oil over the coconut mixture and mix well.

TOMATO DIP

This dip is very quick to make and can be served with any appetiser.

Preparation/Cooking time:
10 minutes

Serving size:
Makes 1 bowl

3 tbsp tomato ketchup
1 tsp vinegar
1 tbsp Chilli Sauce
2 tbsp lime juice
1 small onion grated
1 clove garlic crushed
1 tsp Worcester sauce

1. Mix all the ingredients in a bowl.
2. Keep the Tomato Dip chilled in the fridge till required.

Vegetarian Dishes

QUICK PANEER SALAD

Paneer is a delicious fresh, soft cheese frequently used in Indian cooking.

Preparation/Cooking time:
10 minutes

Serving size:
Serves 4

1 cup paneer cut into cubes

1 cucumber sliced

1 orange peeled and cut into cubes

1 carrot grated

Salad leaves

DRESSING

1 tbsp vinegar
Juice of 1 orange
Crushed black pepper
Salt

1. Place the salad leaves on a serving dish and arrange the paneer, sliced cucumber, orange and grated carrot on top.
2. Mix together all the ingredients for the dressing and pour over the salad.

MIXED YOGURT SALAD

Preparation/Cooking time:
15 minutes

Serving size:
Serves 4

1 cup cabbage shredded

½ cup pineapple cubes

1 apple chopped

1 capsicum (green pepper) finely sliced

1 cup yogurt

1 tbsp almonds, roasted and chopped

1 tsp Chilli Sauce (Pg. 49)

Salt and pepper

For the garnish

1 carrot finely sliced

1 cucumber finely sliced

6 almonds blanched and peeled

2 spring onions

A few olives pitted

1. Add the yogurt, salt and pepper in a bowl and beat until smooth.
2. Add the shredded cabbage, pineapple cubes, apple, capsicum, almonds and Chilli Sauce. Mix well.
3. Decorate with the sliced carrots, cucumber, almonds, spring onions and olives.

PULAO RICE WITH PEAS

Rice is eaten with most Indian meals. Pulao is a tasty variation to plain boiled rice, and may be combined with different spices to vary the taste.

Preparation time:	**Cooking time:**	**Serving size:**
30 minutes	15 minutes	Serves 2

2 cups Basmati rice

200 gm frozen peas

2 onions

4 cloves

2 cinnamon sticks

4 bay leaves

2 tbsp ghee

2 tsp salt

1. Rinse the rice thoroughly and soak in cold water for at least 30 minutes.
2. Heat the ghee in a pan. Chop the onions lengthwise and fry until golden brown. Add the cloves, cinnamon sticks and bay leaves and fry for a few minutes.
3. Add the frozen peas.
4. Drain the rice and add it to the frying pan. Add 2 cups of water to the rice and cover the pan. Boil for about 15-20 minutes until all the water has dried up.
5. Keep the rice covered until it is ready to be served.

SAVOURY PANEER PANCAKES

These delicious pancakes make an easy and filling main course for vegetarians.

Preparation/Cooking time:
30 minutes

Serving size:
8 pancakes

PANCAKES

1 ½ cups milk

100 gm flour

10 gm butter melted

1 tsp salt

Oil for cooking

FILLING

100 gm grated cottage cheese (paneer)

1 cup cubed pineapples

1 onion

4 cloves garlic

4 green chillies (optional)

2 tbsp thick cream

2 tbsp butter

SAUCE

2 tbsp butter

1 onion chopped finely

1 tsp garlic paste

2 bay leaves

FOR THE PANCAKES

1. Mix the milk, flour, butter and salt in a bowl and stir well until the batter is smooth.
2. Heat 1 tsp of oil in a frying pan. Add about 2 tbsp of the batter and spread it on the frying pan to make a pancake (about 6 inches in diameter). Cook the pancake on both sides until it turns golden brown.
3. Repeat the above method to make about 8 pancakes.

FOR THE FILLING

1. Finely chop the onion, garlic and chillies.
2. Melt the butter in a frying pan. Add the chopped onions and fry for about 2 minutes. Add the garlic, chillies, grated paneer and pineapple cubes and cook for about 5 more minutes.
3. Add the cream and bring the mixture to a boil.
4. Turn off the heat and let the filling cool down.
5. Divide the filling into 8 portions. Roll up

1 tsp white pepper
½ cup tomato ketchup
½ cup tomato puree
4 tbsp thick cream
½ cup milk
1 tsp salt
2 tbsp grated cheese

each pancake with the filling and arrange on a baking dish.

FOR THE SAUCE

1. Heat the butter in a pan. Add the chopped onions and fry until brown.
2. Add the garlic paste, tomato ketchup, tomato puree, cream, milk, bay leaves, salt and white pepper. Turn up the heat and simmer for a few minutes.

Pour the sauce over the pancakes. Sprinkle the grated cheese over the top and bake in a hot oven for about 15 minutes. Serve hot.

Savoury Paneer Pancakes

SPINACH KOFTAS

Kofta is the name given to small dough balls or meat balls. In this recipe, the koftas are meat-less. They are made with spinach and stuffed with nuts, raisins and spices to enrich the flavour.

Preparation/Cooking time:
30 minutes

Serving size:
6 portions

KOFTA BALLS

1 kg chopped spinach

3 tbsp gram flour

3 potatoes (boiled and mashed)

2 tbsp chopped cashewnuts

2 tbsp raisins

¼ tsp saffron

1 tsp cardamom powder

1 tsp salt

Oil for frying

1. Boil the spinach in salty water, strain and squeeze out all the water.
2. In a large bowl mix together the spinach, mashed potatoes, gram flour and salt and make a stiff dough.
3. Divide the dough into 12 equal portions and roll into small balls (koftas).
4. In a separate bowl, mix the cashewnuts, raisins, saffron and cardamom powder.
5. Stuff the cashewnut mixture into each kofta.
6. Heat the oil in a frying pan, and deep fry the koftas until they are golden brown in colour.

(continued next page)

Spinach Koftas

GRAVY

½ cup onion paste

½ cup tomato puree

½ cup milk

2 tsp ginger paste

1 tsp garlic paste

1 tsp garam masala

½ tsp cumin powder

1 tsp coriander powder

2 tsp chilli powder (optional)

1 tsp salt

2 tbsp ghee or butter

7. Add the koftas and gravy mixture (see below) into a large saucepan and boil for about 2-3 minutes.
8. Carefully transfer the koftas and gravy into a serving dish and serve hot.

FOR THE GRAVY

1. In a frying pan, heat the ghee and saute the onion paste in it until it turns brown.
2. Add all the remaining ingredients and bring the mixture to a boil. Lower the heat and simmer for about 10 minutes.
3. Follow Steps 7. and 8. above.

CHEESY BAKED CABBAGE

This is a quick and easy recipe that makes for a delicious main dish.

Preparation time:
45 minutes

Serving size:
4 portions

500 gm shredded cabbage
2 tbsp butter
1 tsp grated lemon rind
1 tbsp lemon juice
1 tsp sesame seeds
1 cup White Sauce (Pg. 40)
½ cup grated cheese
A few crushed salty crackers
1 tsp salt

1. Heat the butter in a frying pan. Fry the sesame seeds.
2. Add the shredded cabbage, lemon rind, lemon juice and salt.
3. Cover the pan and cook on low heat for about 5 minutes.
4. Transfer the cooked cabbage into an oven-proof glass dish. Pour the White Sauce over the cabbage, and sprinkle the cheese and crushed crackers on top.
5. Grill in a hot oven for about 15 minutes until the cheese turns brown.
6. Serve hot.

BAKED CAULIFLOWER

This dish uses a perfect East-West blend of flavours - combining Indian spices with traditional White Sauce, which makes it absolutely irresistible.

Preparation/Cooking time:
30 minutes

Serving size:
4 portions

1 cauliflower semi-boiled
½ cup peas boiled
2 onions ground to a paste
3 tomatoes pureed
1 tsp ginger paste
1 tsp garlic paste
1 tsp coriander powder
1 tsp chilli powder (optional)
1 tsp garam masala powder
2 tbsp White Sauce (Pg. 40)
2 tbsp grated cheese
A few crushed potato chips
1 tsp salt
3 tbsp oil

1. Heat the oil in a frying pan and saute the onion paste for 5 minutes.
2. Add the ginger, garlic, chilli powder, coriander powder, garam masala powder, salt, tomato puree and peas and cook for a few minutes.
3. Next add the whole cauliflower and simmer in the gravy for about 5 minutes.
4. Place the cauliflower in a round oven-proof glass dish. Pour all the gravy over the cauliflower.
5. Spread the White Sauce on top and sprinkle the cheese and crushed chips over it.
6. Grill in a hot oven for about 5-7 minutes, until the cheese turns golden brown.
7. Serve Hot.

Baked Cauliflower

SPINACH ROLLS IN TOMATO SAUCE

This recipe has been a favourite of mine whenever I entertain vegetarian guests.

Preparation time:
30 minutes

Serving size:
6-8 portions

12 fresh spinach leaves

½ kg potatoes (boiled, peeled and mashed)

1 large onion chopped

2 green chillies chopped

½ cup boiled corn

1 cup thick cream

1 cup White Sauce (Pg. 40)

1 cup tomato puree strained

2 tbsp grated cheese

2 tbsp butter

2 tbsp oil

Salt

1. Smear the spinach leaves with oil.
2. In a large bowl, combine together the mashed potatoes, onions, chillies, corn, salt and butter.
3. Place 1 spoon of the potato mixture onto a spinach leaf and then roll up the leaf. Repeat until all the spinach leaves are rolled up with the potato fillings.
4. Arrange the spinach rolls on a greased oven-proof glass dish.
5. In a small bowl, mix together the White Sauce, tomato puree, salt and cream and pour the mixture over the spinach rolls.
6. Sprinkle the cheese over the rolls and bake in a preheated moderate oven for about 30-35 minutes.
7. Serve hot.

Spinach Rolls in Tomato Sauce

COLOURFUL POORIS

Poori is the name given to a deep-fried unleavened bread that tastes best when served hot and puffed up.

Preparation time:
40 minutes

Cooking time:
15 minutes

Serving size:
20-25 pooris

2 cups flour
1 beetroot
2 tbsp ghee
1 tsp salt
1 cup milk
Oil for frying

RED POORIS

1. Combine the flour and salt together in a bowl. Add the ghee and rub it in well.
2. Add the beetroot in a saucepan of boiling water and simmer for about 10 minutes, until the beetroot is soft.
3. Mash the beet root and add it to the flour and ghee mixture. Knead well, adding the milk slowly, until the dough is stiff.
4. Cover the bowl with a moist cloth and let it stand for about 20 minutes.
5. Divide the dough into 20-25 portions.
6. Using a rolling pin, roll out each portion into circles of 3 inch diameters.
7. Heat the oil in a saucepan and fry each poori until it puffs up. For best results, start frying only when the oil is very hot.
8. Drain the pooris on absorbent paper and serve immediately.

2 cups flour
100 gm spinach
2 tbsp ghee
1 tsp salt
1 cup milk
Oil for frying

GREEN POORIS

1. Boil and puree the spinach.
2. In a large bowl, combine the flour and salt. Add the ghee and rub it in well.
3. Add the pureed spinach to the flour mixture. Slowly add the milk and knead well until the dough is stiff.
4. Follow steps 4 through 8 above.

Serve as an accompaniment with a main dish, or as colourful snacks with pickles.

CORN AND CHEESE SURPRISE

This sweet corn and bread dish is a perfectly balanced light meal.

Preparation time: 10 minutes

Baking time: 15 minutes

Serving size: Serves 4

2 cups boiled corn

6 tbsp mayonnaise or Garlic Mayonnaise (Pg. 46)

3 tbsp green onions chopped

1 tbsp cream

1 tsp garlic crushed

2 tbsp tomato ketchup

4 tbsp grated Cheddar cheese

4 slices of bread cut diagonally into triangles

Salt and Pepper

Fresh parsley or coriander leaves

1. In a bowl, mix together the corn, mayonnaise, green onions, crushed garlic, tomato ketchup and half the grated cheese.
2. Pour the mixture into a baking dish. Arrange the bread triangles along the edges.
3. Sprinkle the remaining cheese over the bread.
4. Bake in a preheated hot oven for 15 minutes, or until the cheese turns golden brown.
5. Garnish with fresh parsley or coriander leaves.
6. Serve hot.

Serve with Spicy Aubergine Sauce (Pg. 48).

CORN AND PANEER MOUSSAKA

This baked dish looks and tastes terrific and is a perfect way to impress your guests.

Preparation time:
20 minutes

Baking time:
15 minutes

Serving size:
Serves 4

2 cups boiled corn

1 aubergine (brinjal) cut into thin slices and fried

2 potatoes boiled and cut into cubes

2 onions (chopped)

½ cup grated cheese

½ cup tomato ketchup

½ cup White Sauce (Pg. 40)

2 tsp coriander powder

1 tsp cumin powder

½ tsp chilli powder

½ cup paneer cubes

Oil for frying

Salt to taste

1. Heat the oil in a pan and fry the onions until brown.
2. Stir in the potatoes, tomato ketchup, coriander powder, cumin powder, chilli powder and salt.
3. Add pancer cubes to the pan. Cook for 5 minutes.
4. Spread the corn at the bottom of a baking dish.
5. Evenly spread the potato and paneer mixture over it.
6. Arrange the fried aubergine (brinjal) slices on top and pour the White Sauce over it.
7. Sprinkle the grated cheese on top.
8. Bake in a preheated hot oven for about 15 minutes.

VEGETABLE SEEKH KEBABS

Traditionally seekh kebabs are made from a spicy meat mixture, but this version makes a tasty vegetarian alternative.

Preparation/Cooking time:
30 minutes

Serving size:
15 kebabs

1 cup chana dal (yellow lentils)

2 potatoes boiled and mashed

1 tsp garlic paste

1 tsp ginger paste

1 tsp garam masala

1 tsp lemon juice

3 green chillies finely chopped

2 tbsp breadcrumbs

1 tbsp chopped coriander leaves

1 tsp salt

Oil for frying

1 Seekh (barbeque stick about ¼th inch thick)

1. Soak the chana dal for about 4-5 hours. Drain the water and grind the lentils.
2. Combine all the remaining ingredients in a large bowl and mix well.
3. Divide the mixture into 15 equal portions.
4. Grease the seek-stick and wrap one portion of the mixture evenly along the stick to form about a 2-inch long kebab. Gently slide the mixture off the stick and deep fry it in hot oil. Repeat this for all 15 portions.

Serve the kebabs with onion rings and Mint Chutney (Pg. 42).

BAKED AUBERGINES (BRINJAL) WITH CHICKPEAS

Cooking time:
30 minutes

Serving size:
4 portions

2 aubergines (brinjals) cut into 2 inch long cubes

2 onions cut into thick slices

½ cup tomato puree

1 cup chickpeas (soaked and boiled or canned)

Freshly ground pepper

Salt to taste

2 tbsp grated cheese

1 cup oil

1. Heat the oil in a frying pan. Fry the aubergine cubes until they are golden brown on all sides. Drain them on a paper towel.
2. Fry the onions in the same oil till they are just turning brown. Remove the onions from the oil and drain them on a paper towel.
3. Place the fried aubergines and onions in an oven-proof dish.
4. In a bowl, mix together the chickpeas and tomato puree. Season the mixture with freshly ground pepper and salt.
5. Pour the mixture over the aubergine and onions. Sprinkle the grated cheese on top.
6. Place the serving dish under a grill for a few minutes to brown the cheese before serving.
7. Serve hot.

SPICY MACARONI

This makes a really hearty dish.

Cooking time:
20 minutes

Serving size:
2–3 portions

1 cup macaroni

1 cup frozen or boiled peas

1 cup chopped onions

1 cup tomato puree

1 tsp ginger paste

1 tsp garlic paste

½ tsp chilli powder

1 tsp garam masala powder

2 tbsp chopped coriander leaves

Salt to taste

2 tbsp oil

For the garnish

1 tomato sliced

A few coriander leaves

1. Boil the macaroni in salted water according to directions on the packet. Drain and keep aside.
2. Heat the oil and fry the onions till they turn transparent.
3. Add the ginger paste, garlic paste and chilli powder and fry for a few minutes.
4. Next add the tomato puree, boiled macaroni, peas, salt and garam masala. Allow the mixture to simmer for few minutes.
5. Transfer the macaroni onto a serving dish and serve hot.

① Spicy macaroni
② Spicy Bread Rolls—p. 23

VEGETABLE NOODLE CASSEROLE

This recipe makes a nutritious and tasty meal for the whole family.

Preparation time:
15 minutes

Cooking time:
15 minutes

Serving size:
Serves 4

2 cups noodles boiled
2 carrots cut into thin strips
1 cup peas boiled
1 cup cauliflower florets boiled
1 potato boiled and chopped
1 capsicum sliced
1 onion sliced
1 cup cream
2 tbsp tomato ketchup
1 tbsp Chilli Sauce (Pg. 49)
1 tsp garlic crushed
1 tsp crushed black pepper
Salt to taste
1 tbsp oil

1. Heat the oil in a frying pan and add the crushed garlic and black pepper.
2. Add the sliced onions and saute for a few minutes.
3. Add all the remaining ingredients and mix well.
4. Cover the pan and cook for 15-20 minutes.
5. Serve hot.

Vegetable Noodle Casserole

KOFTAS IN COCONUT CURRY

This is a deliciously different way to serve for a special occasion or to liven up a simple meal.

Cooking time:
30 minutes

Serving size:
4 portions

Koftas

6 bread slices

4 boiled potatoes

2 tbsp chopped onions

1 tsp chopped ginger

1 tsp lemon juice

½ tsp garam masala

½ tsp chilli powder

1 tsp salt

½ cup oil

Gravy

2 tbsp chopped onion

½ tsp ginger paste

1 tsp chopped green chillies

½ tsp turmeric powder

2 tsp coriander powder

1 tsp garam masala

1 cup coconut milk

Salt

2 tbsp oil

To make the Koftas

1. Soak the bread slices in water. Then squeeze the bread to take out the extra water.
2. Mash the potatoes.
3. Add the squeezed bread, mashed potatoes and all the ingredients into a bowl and mix well to form a firm dough. Divide the dough into 10–12 equal size balls.
4. Deep fry the dough balls till they turn brown.
5. Drain the fried balls on a paper towel and keep aside.

For the Gravy

1. Heat the oil and sauté the onions till they turn golden brown.
2. Add the ginger paste, chillies, turmeric powder, coriander powder and garam masala. Cook for a few minutes.
3. Finally add coconut milk, bring the mixture to a boil.

To Serve

1. Arrange the dough balls (koftas) on a serving dish.
2. Carefully pour the gravy over the dough balls.
3. Serve hot.

CHEESY CABBAGE AND CORN BAKE

This tasty bake makes a superb meal in itself or it can be served as an accompaniment.

Cooking time:
30 minutes

Serving size:
4 portions

1 cup cabbage (shredded)
1 cup corn (boiled)
2 tbsp butter
1 tbsp lime juice
1 tbsp sesame seeds
½ cup White Sauce (Pg. 40)
2 tbsp grated cheese
Salt

1. Heat the butter and fry the sesame seeds.
2. Add the cabbage and cook it for a few minutes. Add the corn, salt and lime juice.
3. Transfer the mixture to an oven proof dish.
4. Pour the White Sauce over the mixture and sprinkle the grated cheese on top.
5. Place the dish under the grill for 15-20 minutes until the cheese turns brown.
6. Serve hot.

MINTY AUBERGINE (BRINJAL) SHELLS

In this recipe the aubergines are stuffed with vegetables and spices to make a delicious and filling meal.

Cooking time:
40 minutes

Serving size:
4 portions

2 large aubergines (brinjals)
2 onions (chopped)
2 tomatoes (chopped)
2 potatoes boiled and chopped
½ cup peas (boiled)
½ cup curd
1 tsp garlic paste
1 tsp chilli paste
1 tsp garam masala
3 tbsp oil
Salt

To serve
1 bunch mint leaves chopped
½ cup beaten curd (Yogurt)

1. Cut the brinjals in half lengthwise and remove the flesh leaving about ½ inch thick shells. Brush the shells with oil.
2. Chop the scooped brinjal flesh.
3. Heat the oil in a pan and fry the onions along with the chopped brinjal flesh.
4. Add the tomatoes, garlic, chilli paste and continue to fry for a few minutes.
5. Add all the remaining ingredients and mix well.
6. Fill in the mixture into the brinjal shells.
7. Place the stuffed shells on a serving dish and bake in preheated hot oven for 30 minutes.

To serve
Spread the beaten curd and mint leaves on top of the hot brinjal shells and serve immediately.

RIPE BANANA CURRY

This curry can be made very quickly and served as a side dish as well as a main course.

Cooking time:
20 minutes

Serving size:
3-4 portions

3 ripe bananas
3 tbsp onion paste
4 tbsp tomato puree
¼ tsp turmeric powder
½ tsp cumin seed powder
½ tsp red chilli powder
3 tbsp yogurt (curd)
½ cup water
3 tbsp oil
Salt

To serve
1 tbsp coriander (chopped)
1 green chilli (chopped)
½ tsp garam masala

1. Peel and cut each banana into 2 or 3 pieces.
2. Heat the oil and lightly fry the bananas. Keep aside.
3. In the same oil fry the onions till brown.
4. Add all the dry spices, tomato puree and yogurt and keep frying till the oil starts to separate. Add ½ cup water and let the mixture boil for 5 minutes.
5. Add the bananas and simmer for 5 more minutes.
6. Sprinkle the chopped coriander, chillies and garam masala. Serve hot with Colourful Pooris (Pg. 68).

PANEER & CAPSICUM SUBZI

Cooking time:
15 minutes

Serving size:
2 portions

250 gm paneer
1 cup milk
1 tbsp butter
1 tbsp flour
2 tbsp tomato ketchup
1 tsp Chilli Sauce (Pg. 49)
1 capsicum (green pepper) cut into thin strips
1 onion chopped
Salt and pepper

1. Heat the butter in a pan and fry the onions till light brown.
2. Add the capsicum and saute for few seconds.
3. Add the flour and stir for 1 minute, then add the tomato ketchup and Chilli Sauce.
4. Add the milk slowly, stirring continuously till it starts to simmer.
5. Finally add the paneer cubes, salt and pepper. Allow the mixture to boil for about 1 minute before removing the pan from the heat. Serve hot.

TOMATO RICE

For this recipe you may use 2 cups of boiled spaghetti instead of the rice. I have also suggested a Chicken variation for non-vegetarians.

Cooking time:
15 minutes

Serving size:
2 portions

2 tea cups boiled rice
1 cup mixed vegetables: carrots, peas and corn
2 chopped onions
1 tbsp crushed garlic (or paste)
1 chopped capsicum (green peppers)
1 cup tomato ketchup
2 tbsp Chilli Sauce (Pg. 49)
2 tbsp vinegar or lime juice
3 tbsp oil
Salt and pepper to taste
(diced chicken)

1. Heat the oil and fry the onions till golden brown. Add the capsicum and garlic and stir for about 2 minutes.
2. Add the ketchup, Chilli Sauce and vinegar.
3. Add the rice, vegetables, salt and pepper, and cook for about 1 minute.
4. Transfer the rice to a serving dish and serve hot.

Variation: Fry the onions till golden brown. Add the CHICKEN and cook for 8/9 minutes.

Fish & Meat Dishes

CHICKEN IN SHERRY

This easy dish is always a hit. Double the quantities if you are cooking for a larger group.

Cooking time:
30 minutes

Serving Size:
4 portions

4 chicken pieces
1 tsp garlic paste
1 tsp ginger paste
¼ tsp ground black pepper
¼ tsp Chilli Sauce (Pg. 49)
2 tsp lime juice
½ cup sherry
1 tbsp butter
Salt

1. Mix together all the ingredients, except the butter, and marinate the chicken in it.
2. Heat the butter in a pan and cook the chicken till it is tender.
3. Place the chicken on a dish and serve hot.

CREAMED PRAWNS IN RICE RING

This is a tasty and filling dish that is spicy and creamy.

Preparation/Cooking time:
20 minutes

Serving size:
2 portions

250 gm prawns (shelled)

2 tbsp butter

1 onion finely chopped

1 tbsp flour

1 cup milk

10 peppercorns

2 bay leaves

3 tbsp thick cream

2 tbsp grated Cheddar cheese

Salt and pepper

1 tomato sliced (to decorate)

FOR THE RICE RING

250 gms rice

2 tbsp butter or oil

3 cubes chicken stock

6 cups water

1 tsp salt

1. Mix the flour, half the butter and milk in a bowl to make White Sauce (Pg 40). Stir in the cream and the cheese.
2. Heat the remaining butter in a frying pan. Add the onions and saute until they turn brown.
3. Stir in the prawns and cook for a few minutes.
4. Add the White Sauce and cheese mixture to the prawns and heat gently. Add the salt and pepper according to taste.
5. For the rice ring, boil the water with the chicken stock cubes and rice. When the rice is cooked, drain the extra water. Mix in the butter and salt and arrange the rice around the sides of a serving dish.
6. Pour the creamed prawns in the centre of the serving dish. Decorate with sliced tomatoes.
7. Serve hot.

PRAWN KEBABS

Cooking time:
25 minutes

Serving size:
12 to 15 pieces

700 gm prawns cleaned
1 tsp ginger paste
1 tsp garlic paste
2 tbsp flour
2 tbsp breadcrumbs
2 onions chopped
2 green chillies chopped (optional)
½ tsp chilli powder
½ tsp salt
½ tsp black salt
½ tsp pepper
1 egg
Oil for frying

To serve
1 onion (medium size)
1 tomato
1 cucumber
Juice of one lime
½ tsp salt
2 tbsp coriander leaves (chopped)

1. Chop the prawns and add all the ingredients and knead well.
2. Shape the mixture into 2 inch long kebabs.
3. Heat the oil in a frying pan and deep fry all the kebabs. Place the kebabs on a paper towel to soak the excess oil.

To serve
1. Chop the remaining onions, cucumber and tomato into thin long slices.
2. In another frying pan, heat 1 tsp oil and add all the chopped vegetables, chopped coriander, lime juice and salt. Saute for a few minutes.
3. Place the sautéed vegetables on a serving dish and arrange the fried prawns over them. Serve hot.

FISH PUNJABI

A popular Indian variation of the traditional English Fish and Chips, using gram flour and spices.

Preparation/Cooking time:
20 minutes plus
1 hour marinating time

Serving size:
4 portions

8 fish fillets
1 tbsp lemon juice
25 gm Besan (Gram flour)
1 egg
½ tsp ground black pepper
½ tsp turmeric powder
1 tsp chilli powder (optional)
1 tsp cardamom powder
½ tsp ajwain (thyme)
½ tsp garlic paste
½ tsp ginger paste
1 tsp salt
Oil for frying

1. Wash the fish fillets and pat dry.
2. Mix together all the remaining ingredients to form a thick batter.
3. Marinate the fish in it for at least 1 hour.
4. Deep fry the fish with the batter and serve hot.

SERVING SUGGESTION

Serve with sliced lemon and green chillies on a bed of potato chips, along with spicy Date Chutney (Pg. 45).

GRILLED GARLIC CHICKEN

Preparation/Cooking time:
20 minutes plus
1 hour marinating time

Baking time:
20-25 minutes

Serving size:
4 portions

4 chicken breast fillets

6 cloves of garlic crushed

1 tbsp crushed peppercorns

2 tbsp finely chopped coriander leaves

2 tbsp lemon juice

2 tsp salt

1 tbsp oil

1. In a bowl, mix together the crushed garlic, peppercorns, lemon juice, salt and coriander leaves. Rub the mixture over the chicken fillets. Cover and keep in the refrigerator for about 1 hour.
2. Place the chicken on a baking tray and grill in hot oven for about 20 minutes until the chicken fully cooked.

Serve hot with Garlic Mayonnaise (Pg. 46).

CHUTNEY FISH

This fish has an aroma of mint chutney and a rich creamy taste.

Preparation time:
30 minutes plus
30 minutes marinating time

Serving size:
4 portions

500 gm fish fillets

1 medium onion (chopped)

6 tbsp Mint Chutney (Pg. 42)

½ cup half and half cream

2 tbsp oil

1 tbsp lemon juice

1 tsp salt

1. Mix the lemon juice and salt in a small bowl. Marinate the fish in it for 30 minutes.
2. Heat the oil in a shallow frying pan. Add the onions and fry until they turn brown.
3. Add the fish fillets and cook for about 5 minutes on each side.
4. Add the chutney and cream and simmer for 2-3 minutes.
5. Serve hot.

FISH PIES WITH MUSTARD SAUCE

Preparation time:
30 minutes

Serving size:
Makes 8 pies

PIE CRUST

1 cup flour

50 gm butter

1 bowl of cold water

Oil for frying

FILLING

1 cup flaked cooked fish

¼ cup mayonnaise

1 small onion finely chopped

1 tbsp tomato sauce

1 tbsp Chilli Sauce (optional)

1 tbsp coriander leaves (chopped)

1 tbsp roasted crushed peanuts

TOPPING

1 tomato thinly sliced

A few mint leaves

1. Rub the butter into the flour adding about 5 table spoons of cold water to make a soft dough.
2. Divide the dough into 16 portions. Using a rolling pin, roll out each portion into circles of 3 inch diameters.
3. In a large bowl, mix all the ingredients for the filling.
4. Place about 1 spoonful of the filling in the centre of a dough circle. Wet the sides of the circle with some water. Place another dough circle on top and seal the edges of the pie with a fork.
5. Repeat step 4. for all 8 pies.
6. Heat the oil in a frying pan and fry the pies carefully for about 5-6 minutes each.
7. Place the pies on some paper towels to drain the oil.
8. Arrange the pies on a serving dish. Place a slice of tomato and a mint leaf on each pie.

Serve hot with Mustard Sauce (Pg. 47).

TRADITIONAL CHICKEN CURRY

No Indian cook book would be complete without this traditional curried dish from northern India.

Preparation/Cooking time:
30 minutes

Serving size:
4 portions

1 kg chicken
100 gm vegetable oil
2 large cardamoms
2 cinnamon sticks
6 cloves
10 black pepper corns
2 onions chopped
1 tsp ginger paste
1 tsp garlic paste
½ tsp turmeric powder
100 gm chopped tomatoes
2 tsp salt
50 gm ground cashewnuts
100 gm milk
2 tsp chopped coriander leaves

1. Wash the chicken and cut into 3 inch pieces.
2. Heat the oil in a large frying pan. Add the pepper corns, cardamoms, cinnamon and cloves. Cook for about 2 minutes.
3. Add the onions and fry until they turn brown.
4. Add the turmeric powder, ginger paste, garlic paste and chopped tomatoes.
5. Bring the mixture to a boil, turn down the heat and simmer for about 15 minutes.
6. Add the chicken and the salt. Cook for a further 15-20 minutes, stirring continuously, until the chicken is tender.
7. Add the milk and cashewnuts and simmer for a few minutes.
8. Sprinkle the coriander leaves on top before serving.

CHEESY BAKED FISH

This nourishing baked dish is just the right thing for a healthy dinner.

Preparation/ Cooking time:
45 minutes

Baking time:
25-30 minutes

Serving size:
4 portions

500 gm fish fillets
8 slices cheddar cheese
4 tbsp Garlic Mayonnaise (Pg. 46)
1 onion (chopped)
1 clove garlic crushed
1 cup tomato puree
½ cup chicken stock
2 tsp butter
2 tbsp breadcrumbs
Salt and pepper
1 sliced tomato
Fresh coriander or parsley

1. Spread the Garlic Mayonnaise on each fish fillet.
2. Heat the butter in a frying pan and saute the onions until brown. Add the crushed garlic, chicken stock, tomato puree, salt and pepper and cook until the mixture is thick.
3. Arrange 4 slices of cheese on a greased baking dish. Place the fish fillets over it, and then place the remaining cheese slices on top.
4. Pour the tomato mixture around the fish and cheese and sprinkle the breadcrumbs over it.
5. Bake in a moderate oven for 25-30 minutes.
6. Decorate with sliced tomatoes and fresh coriander or parsley. Serve hot.

Cheesy Baked Fish

CHICKEN KEBABS

Preparation/Cooking time:
45 minutes
plus marinating time

Serving size:
6 portions

500 gm boneless chicken cut into 1 inch cubes

Juice of 1 lemon

6 cloves garlic

1 inch long ginger

2 tsp vinegar

1 cup thick yogurt

1 tsp salt

½ tsp tandoori powder

2 onions

1 capsicum

2 tomatoes

Toothpicks or skewers

1. Place the chicken cubes in a bowl and mix in the lemon juice and salt. Keep aside for 15 minutes.
2. Grind the ginger and garlic. Mix together with the yogurt, vinegar and tandoori powder to form a thick paste.
3. Pour the paste over the chicken cubes and mix well. Marinate the chicken in the refrigerator for about 4-6 hours.
4. Cut the capsicum and tomatoes into 1 inch squares.
5. Slide one piece of chicken, tomato and capsicum on each toothpick. Use 3 pieces of each if using skewers.
6. Arrange the toothpicks/skewers on a baking tray and grill in a moderate oven for about 20-25 minutes.
7. Serve over Pulao Rice with Peas (Pg. 56) or with fresh salad.

① Pulao Rice with Peas—p. 56
② Chicken Kebabs

BAKED CHICKEN 'N RICE

This dish makes a tasty dinner and is very simple to cook.

Preparation/ Cooking time: 20 minutes

Baking time: 20-25 minutes

Serving size: 2 portions

2 cups cooked basmati rice
1 cup cooked chicken cubed
½ cup grated cheddar cheese
½ cup sliced mushrooms
¼ cup single cream
¼ cup White Sauce (Pg. 40)
2 tsp chopped parsley
1 tsp salt
1 tsp pepper

1. In a large bowl, combine all the ingredients (except the rice and cheese) and mix well.
2. Slowly add the rice and mix gently.
3. Transfer the mixture to a baking dish and bake covered in a moderate oven for about 20 minutes.
4. Remove the dish from the oven and sprinkle the cheese over the top of the chicken and rice mixture.
5. Bake uncovered for about 5 minutes more or until the cheese melts.

CHICKEN NOODLE CREPES

These delicious stuffed crepes make a healthy meal and are enjoyed by children and grown ups alike.

Preparation time:
40 minutes

Serving size:
8 portions

CREPES

1½ cups milk

100 gm flour

10 gm butter

1 tsp salt

Oil for frying

FILLING

1 cup boiled noodles

½ cup chicken boiled and diced

½ cup cabbage chopped

½ cup spring onions chopped

1 carrot grated

1 capsicum (green pepper) thinly sliced

4 cloves garlic crushed

2 tsp soya sauce

2 tsp vinegar

½ tsp salt

2 tbsp oil

Tomato ketchup

Chilli Sauce (Optional–Pg. 49)

FOR THE CREPES

1. Mix the milk, flour, salt and butter in a bowl and stir well until the batter is smooth.
2. Heat 1 tsp of oil in a frying pan. Add about 1 tbsp of the batter and spread it on the frying pan to make a crepe about 6 inches in diameter. Cook the crepe on both sides until it turns golden brown.

Repeat the above method to make about 8 crepes.

FOR THE FILLING

1. Heat the oil in a frying pan. Add the crushed garlic and all the vegetables and saute for a few minutes.
2. Add the diced chicken, soya sauce, vinegar and salt.
3. Add in the noodles and mix well.

TO SERVE

1. Spread two spoonfuls of the chicken and noodle filling along the centre of each crepe.
2. Drizzle some Chilli Sauce (optional) and tomato ketchup over the filling.
3. Roll up the crepes and place on a serving dish.

SERVING SUGGESTION

Serve warm with fresh salad.

CORIANDER CHICKEN WITH MAYONNAISE

Cooking time:
40 minutes

Serving size:
2-3 portions

500 gm chicken cut into pieces

2 tbsp butter

2 tbsp chopped green onions

1 tsp garlic paste

1 tsp coriander powder

½ tsp chilli powder

½ cup white wine

Salt to taste

2 tbsp chopped coriander leaves

1 cup mayonnaise

1. Heat the butter in a frying pan. Add the chicken pieces and brown well on both sides.
2. Add the chopped onions, garlic paste, coriander powder, chilli powder, salt and wine. Cover the pan and simmer over low heat until the chicken is tender.
3. Generously spread the mayonnaise on the bottom of a serving dish.
4. Place the hot chicken over the mayonnaise and sprinkle the chopped coriander leaves on top. Serve immediately.

LAMB BIRYANI

Biryani is a traditional rice dish that is typically eaten on special occasions. This recipe is a simplified version of the traditional biryani, but it is just as tasty.

Preparation time:
40 minutes plus marinating time

Serving size:
6 portions

- 1 kg lamb cut into 2 inch pieces (with the bone)
- ½ cup yogurt
- 500 gm basmati rice
- 6 onions chopped
- 6 cloves garlic
- 2 inch ginger
- 2 bay leaves
- 2 cinnamon sticks
- 2 tsp amchur (mango powder)
- 1 tsp garam masala
- 2 tsp salt
- 2 tbsp oil
- 3 cups water
- ½ tsp saffron (soaked in 2 tbsp rose water)

1. Grind together the ginger, garlic and 1 tsp salt and mix with the yogurt. Marinate the lamb pieces in this mixture overnight, or for at least 4 hours.
2. Heat the oil in a frying pan and add the bay leaves and cinnamon sticks. Add the onions and saute until they are brown.
3. Add the remaining ingredients along with the lamb and cook for about 30 minutes, or until it is tender.
4. In a separate pan, boil the rice in water and 1 tsp salt for about 15 minutes until all the water has dried up.
5. Place the rice and meat in a baking dish. Mix in the saffron and bake covered in a moderate oven for 30 minutes.
6. Serve hot with Yogurt Dip (Pg. 50).

PICKLED LAMB CURRY

This delicious curry may be served hot or cold.

Preparation time:
40 minutes

Serving size:
6-8 portions

1 kg lamb cut into 1 inch cubes
3 onions chopped
2 tsp ground ginger paste
2 tsp garlic paste
2 cups mustard oil
2 tbsp chilli powder (optional)
1 tbsp mango powder
1 tbsp cumin seeds
6 black cardamoms
12 cloves
2 sticks cinnamon
Salt to taste

Pickled Lamb Curry

1. Add the lamb cubes into a large saucepan and simmer without adding any water, until all the liquid from the meat runs outs and dries up. Set aside.
2. Heat the mustard oil in a frying pan and add the cumin seeds, cardamoms, cloves and cinnamon sticks.
3. Next, add the onions, ginger and garlic paste and fry for about 5 minutes.
4. Add the lamb cubes and continue to fry, mixing well.
5. Add all the remaining ingredients and cook for a further 5 minutes, stirring continuously.
6. Remove the lamb curry from the heat and transfer to a serving dish. Refrigerate for at least 4 hours if serving cold.

FRIED FISH TIKKA

A simple dish—good as a snack or a main course.

Preparation time:	**Cooking time:**	**Serving Size:**
3-4 hours marination	20 minutes	4–6 portions

500 gm boneless fish cut into 2″ pieces
1 tbsp lime juice
1 tbsp vinegar
1 tbsp cornflour
1 tsp coriander powder
1 tsp chilli powder
1 tsp mango powder
1 tsp garam masala
1 tsp ginger paste
1 tsp garlic paste
Salt to taste
Oil for frying

For the garnish:
1 tsp Chat Masala
1 onion cut into fine rings

1. Mix all the spices and marinate the fish for 3-4 hours.
2. Heat the oil and deep fry the fish pieces.
3. Sprinkle the Chat Masala on the fish. Arrange the onion rings and the fish on a serving dish and serve hot.

Fried Fish Tikka

FRIED LAMB CHOPS

Preparation time:
40 minutes

Serving size:
4 portions

500 gm lamb chops
500 ml milk
6 cloves
6 bay leaves
8 cardamoms
1 inch long ginger
1 tbsp aniseeds
10 peppercorns
1 tsp salt
1 tsp chilli powder (optional)
Oil for frying

BATTER
140 gms besan (gram flour)
A pinch of saffron
1 tbsp melted ghee or butter
1 tbsp coriander powder
½ tsp garam masala powder
1 tsp salt
¼ tsp baking powder
½ cup water

FOR THE CHOPS

1. Boil the chops in milk.
2. Place all the spices in a muslin bag. Tie the bag securely and place it in the boiling milk for 15 minutes.
3. Remove the muslin bag and grind together all the cooked spices to make a thick paste.
4. Coat the cooked lamb with the spices.

FOR THE BATTER

1. Mix together all the ingredients of the batter in a large bowl. Stir well until the batter thickens.

TO SERVE

1. Dip the lamb chops in the batter. Completely coat each lamb chop with the batter.
2. Fry the lamb chops in oil until they turn golden brown.
3. Serve hot with Chilli Sauce (Pg. 49).

SPICY MEAT BALLS

Cooking time:
45 minutes including
30 minutes chilling time

Serving Size:
15–20 meatballs

250 gm minced lamb
1 slice bread
1 egg
3 tbsp milk
2 tbsp chopped onion
1 tbsp chopped coriander leaves
1 tsp chopped green chillies
½ pod garlic crushed
½ tsp garam masala
½ tsp green cardamom powder
Salt
Oil for frying

1. Soak the bread in the milk.
2. In a large bowl mix together the minced lamb, the egg, the soaked bread and all the remaining ingredients.
3. Shape the mixture into small balls and chill in the refrigerator for about 30 minutes.
4. Heat the oil and fry the meatballs for 10-15 minutes.
5. Drain the oil and arrange the meatballs on a serving dish.
6. Serve hot with Tomato Dip (Pg. 52).

CREAMY LAMB KEBABS

Cooking time:
45 minutes

Serving size:
4 portions

500 gm minced lamb
½ cup cream
2 tbsp cornflour
1 egg
1 tsp coriander powder
1 tsp chilli powder
1 tsp garam masala
1 tsp mango powder (amchur)
1 tsp garlic paste
1 tsp ginger paste
1 tsp chopped coriander leaves
1 tsp chopped green chillies
Salt to taste
4 tbsp oil

1. Mix all the ingredients with the minced meat (except the cream) and knead till it becomes sticky.
2. Divide the mixture into 12 portions and make round patties (wet your hands while making kebabs otherwise the mixture will stick to the hands).
3. Heat the oil in a flat pan, add the kebabs and reduce the heat.
4. Cook the kebabs on both sides for about 20-25 minutes.
5. Arrange the kebabs on a baking dish and pour the cream over them.
6. Place in a hot oven for 5 minutes and serve immediately.

LAMB KOFTA CURRY

Kofta is the Indian name for small dough balls or meat balls. These lamb koftas are an Indian variation of the traditional Swedish meatballs.

Preparation time:
40 minutes

Serving size:
Makes 16 koftas

500 gm minced lamb
50 gm thick plain yogurt
2 large onions (finely chopped)
4 cloves garlic crushed
4 tsp coriander powder
1 tsp chilli powder (optional)
1 tsp salt
4 cups water

GRAVY
4 onions ground to a paste
2 inch ginger ground
10 almonds blanched and ground
2 tsp poppy seeds ground
2 tsp grated coconut
2 tsp garam masala powder
4 tsp coriander powder
1 tsp salt
250 gm ghee or butter
1 cup water

FOR THE KOFTAS

1. Boil the minced lamb and water together with the chopped onions, garlic, coriander powder, chilli powder and salt.
2. When the meat is cooked, drain the water completely and add the yogurt. Mix thoroughly.
3. Make 16 round kofta balls.

FOR THE GRAVY

1. Heat the ghee or butter in a pan.
2. Add all the ingredients for the gravy and saute until the mixture turns brown.
3. Add the water to the mixture, and when it starts to boil, gently add the koftas.
4. Serve hot.

LAMB/MUTTON CHOPS

Cooking time:
40 minutes

Serving size:
4 portions

500 gm lamb/mutton chops
2 cups milk
8 green cardamoms
2 tsp fennel seeds
6 cloves
4 bay leaves
10 pepper corns
1 inch ginger
Salt to taste

For the garnish:
A pinch of saffron soaked in
2 tbsp rose water

1. Boil the chops in the milk along with all the remaining ingredients tied in a muslin bag. Cook until the lamb is tender.
2. Remove the muslin bag and place all the cooked spices in a blender. Grind the spices to a fine paste.
3. Coat the chops with the ground spice paste.
4. Arrange the chops on a serving dish and sprinkle them with rose water and saffron before serving.

TANGY FISH WITH GARLIC POTATOES

Cooking time:
30 minutes plus 1 hour marination

Serving size:
6 portions

For the Fish:
6 fish fillets
1 tbsp soya sauce
1 tbsp tomato sauce
1 tsp Chilli Sauce (Pg. 49)
1 tbsp lime juice
1 tsp vinegar
1 tbsp cornflour
2 tbsp butter

For the Garlic Potatoes:
200 gm boiled potatoes (small size)
1 tbsp butter
4 cloves garlic crushed
Freshly ground pepper and salt

For the garnish:
1 tbsp chopped coriander leaves

To make the Fish

1. Combine all the ingredients and marinate the fish in it for an hour.
2. Heat the butter in a non-stick pan and shallow fry the fish.

To make the Garlic Potatoes

1. Heat the butter in a frying pan. Add the garlic and stir for a few minutes.
2. Add the potatoes, sprinkle the salt and pepper over them and cook on high heat till the potatoes are browned on all sides.

To Serve

Place the fish in a serving dish and arrange the garlic potatoes along the sides. Add the chopped coriander on top and serve hot.

PRAWNS IN CASHEWNUT GRAVY

This creamy dish has a mild nutty flavour.

Cooking time:
40 minutes

Serving size:
4 portions

1 kg prawns cleaned and de-veined
100 gm onions chopped
100 gm tomatoes chopped
1 tsp ginger paste
2 whole green chillies (optional)
1 tsp cumin seed powder
1 tsp salt
½ tsp pepper powder
½ tsp turmeric powder
20 cashewnuts (ground to a paste with a little milk)
½ cup milk
2 tbsp oil

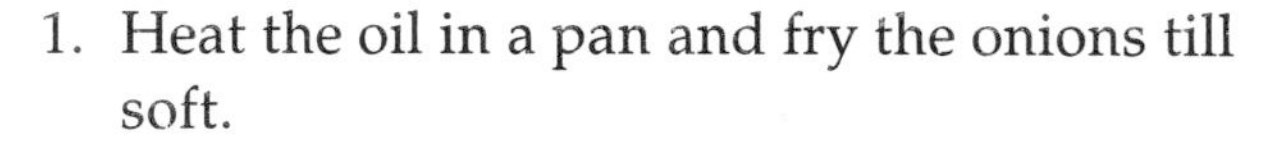

1. Heat the oil in a pan and fry the onions till soft.
2. Add the prawns and green chillies and stir for about 5 minutes.
3. Add the ginger paste, turmeric, salt and pepper and cook on a slow heat for another 15 minutes.
4. Mix in the ground cashewnut and milk paste and simmer for 2-3 minutes.
5. Sprinkle the cumin seed powder on top and serve hot.
6. Garnish with chopped coriander leaves and lemon slices.

Prawns in Cashewnut Gravy

PRAWN COCKTAILS

Very simple to make and remains a family favourite.

Preparation time:
5 minutes plus chilling time

Serving size:
2 portions

- 100 gm prawns (shelled and boiled)
- 3 tbsp mayonnaise sauce
- 2 tbsp tomato ketchup
- 2 tbsp w ipped cream
- ½ tsp Tabasco Sauce or Chilli Sauce (Pg. 49)
- Salt and pepper
- Mint leaves or spring onion tassels (optional)
- 2 cocktail glasses

1. Add all the ingredients into a bowl and mix well.
2. Transfer the mixture into the serving glasses and place a mint leaf or spring onion tassel on top of each glass.
3. Serve chilled.

Prawn Cocktails

GRILLED FISH WITH SPRING ONIONS

For a vegetarian option, replace the fish fillets with paneer slices to make a tasty vegetarian meal.

Cooking time:
20 minutes

Serving Size:
4 portions

500 gm fish fillets

100 gm spring onions chopped

1 tbsp soft butter

½ tsp garlic paste

½ tsp chilli paste

½ inch long ginger peeled and slivered

2 tbsp soya sauce

1 tbsp vinegar

½ tsp sugar

salt

For the garnish:
A few spring onion tassels

1. Mix together the butter, garlic paste, chilli paste and salt. Spread this mixture on both sides of the fish fillets.
2. Arrange the fish fillets in a 1 inch deep baking dish. Scatter some spring onions and ginger over the fish.
3. Mix together the soya sauce, vinegar and sugar and spoon the mixture over the fish.
4. Place the fish under a hot grill for 10-12 minutes.
5. Garnish with spring onion tassels before serving.

CREAMY BAKED CHICKEN

Cooking time:
1 hour

Serving size:
4 portions

4 skinless chicken breasts
4 slices cheese
1 can Cream of Chicken soup (or 1 packet chicken soup)
¼ cup white wine
½ cup breadcrumbs
2 tbsp melted butter
½ tsp garlic powder
2 tbsp grated parmesan cheese

1. Arrange the chicken breasts in a greased baking pan. Top each breast with a cheese slice.
2. In a small bowl, combine the chicken soup and white wine. Stir well. Pour this sauce over the chicken.
3. Sprinkle breadcrumbs over the sauce and drizzle the melted butter over the top. Sprinkle some garlic powder and grated cheese over it.
4. Bake the chicken breasts for 45-55 minutes until the sauce is bubbling. Serve hot.

LAMB IN BEER

Cooking time:
45 minutes

Serving size:
4 portions

1 kg boneless lamb
½ litre beer
2 onion sliced thinly
1 tsp ginger paste
2 bay leaves
2 tsp salt
1 tsp pepper crushed
2 tbsp oil
Few strands of saffron

1. Heat the oil in a pan. Add the crushed peppers, bay leaves and sliced onions and fry till the mixture browns.
2. Add the lamb meat and stir for 2 minutes.
3. Add the ginger paste, salt and beer. Cover the pan with a lid and cook on medium heat for 30 minutes or till the meat is done.
4. Sprinkle the saffron strands on top and serve hot with rice or bread.

SESAME OVEN FRIED CHICKEN

Chicken flavoured with seasame seeds for a nutty taste—which is a true delight.

Cooking time:
40 minutes

Serving size:
4 portions

1 kg chicken boneless cut into 2 inch pieces
1 egg
¼ cup milk
1 tsp Chilli Sauce (Pg. 49)
½ tsp garlic paste
4 tbsp flour
½ tsp garam masala
½ tsp baking powder
2 tbsp seasame seeds
Salt
4 tbsp butter melted

1. In a bowl, beat together the egg, milk, Chilli Sauce and garlic paste. Marinate the chicken in this mixture for 15 minutes.
2. In a separate bowl, combine the flour, garam masala, baking powder, sesame seeds and salt. Coat the marinated chicken pieces with the flour mixture and arrange them on a flat baking dish.
3. Spread half the butter evenly over the chicken.
4. Place the chicken in a medium oven for 15 minutes.
5. Remove the dish from the oven and flip over all the chicken pieces. Spread the remaining butter over the chicken and place the dish back in the oven for another 15 minutes.
6. Serve with Yogurt Dip (Pg. 50).

SAUSAGES IN WHITE SAUCE

Cooking time:
30 minutes

Serving size:
Serves 4

6 potatoes boiled
6 large sausages
2 tbsp butter
1 cup White Sauce (Pg. 40)
½ cup grated cheese
½ tsp garam masala
Salt and Pepper
1 tsp lemon juice

1. Mash the potatoes and season them with salt, pepper, garam masala and lemon juice.
2. Heat the butter in a saucepan and gently fry the sausages.
3. Spread the mashed potatoes on the bottom of an oven-proof dish.
4. Slice the sausages in half length wise and arrange them over the mashed potatoes.
5. Pour the White Sauce over the sausages and sprinkle the grated cheese on top.
6. Grill in a moderate oven for 15 minutes and serve hot.

Desserts & Drinks

PEPPERMINT AND CHERRY SOUFFLE

An attractive looking dessert with a minty flavour.

Preparation time:	**Freezing time:**	**Serving size:**
20 minutes	30 minutes	6 portions

2 eggs
½ cup sugar
2 tsp gelatine
2 tbsp cold water
1 cup cream, whipped
1 bar milk chocolate grated
½ cup canned cherries
Peppermint essence
Green food colouring

1. Add the gelatine and cold water in bowl. Hold the bowl over some boiling water and mix well until the gelatine is dissolved.
2. In a separate bowl, whip the eggs and sugar until the mixture is thick.
3. Add the dissolved gelatine and a few drops of peppermint essence and green food colouring.
4. Fold in the whipped cream.
5. Lightly fold in the cherries and grated chocolate. Remember to keep aside some of the cherries, grated chocolate and whipped cream for decorating the souffle.
6. Pour the mixture into a glass serving dish and put in the refrigerator to set.
7. Once set, decorate the souffle and serve.

SULTANA-WALNUT ICE-CREAM ROLL

In this recipe, almonds may be substituted for walnuts - both work just as well.

Preparation time:
25 minutes

Serving size:
8 portions

CAKE
125 gm sugar
5 eggs
50 gm flour
50 gm cornflour
25 gm cocoa
1 swiss roll tin (13 inches × 9 inches)

FILLING
1 brick vanilla ice cream
3 tbsp sultanas
2 tbsp walnuts, chopped

1. Separate the egg yolks and the egg whites.
2. Beat together the egg yolks and the sugar. Fold in the flour and mix well.
3. Beat the egg whites separately until they are stiff. Then fold the egg whites into the mixture.
4. Pour the mixture into the swiss roll tin lined with wax paper. (Do not grease the tin).
5. Place the tin in the middle shelf of a preheated moderate oven, and bake for about 15 minutes.
6. Cool the cake on a wire rack.
7. Slice the ice-cream thinly and spread over the entire cake. Sprinkle the sultanas and nuts over the ice-cream.
8. Carefully roll the cake and place it on a glass serving dish.
9. Keep the cake in the freezer and cut into slices before serving.

ORANGE KULFI

Kulfi is a milk-based ice-cream that is very popular in India. Typically, Kulfi is made with pistachios and almonds but this variation of the recipe uses oranges instead.

Preparation time:
25 minutes
plus 2-3 hours chilling time

Serving size:
4 portions

4 cups milk
4 oranges
50 gm sugar
4-5 drops of rose water

TOPPING
1 tbsp chopped pistachios

1. Boil the milk for about 15 minutes.
2. Stir in the sugar and rose water and set aside to cool.
3. Peel the oranges. Separate each segment removing the skin and seeds.
4. Arrange the oranges in a glass bowl and pour the milk over it.
5. Freeze it for 2-3 hours, or until firm.

Sprinkle some chopped pistachios over the ice-cream before serving.

ORANGE CHEESE CAKE

This cheese cake takes some time to prepare and cook, but it is well worth the effort. The oranges give it a wonderfully tangy flavour.

Preparation time:
25 minutes plus
2-3 hours chilling time

Serving size:
6 portions

1 packet orange jelly
1 cup water
250 gm plain thick yogurt or plain cream cheese
½ cup castor sugar
1 cup whipped cream
1 tsp finely grated orange rind
10 ginger biscuits
4 tbsp butter
2 oranges
A round 8 inch baking dish with a detachable base

1. Crush the ginger biscuits in a bowl, and mix well with the butter. Transfer the biscuit mixture into the cake dish. Press the mixture with a wooden spoon until it forms a hardened base. Place the dish in the refrigerator to chill.
2. Make the orange jelly according to the instructions on the packet (but use only 1 cup of water) and allow it to set.
3. Whip together the cream and sugar.
4. In a separate bowl, whip together the yogurt and jelly and strain the mixture to make it smooth. Add the orange rind to the mixture.
5. Fold in the whipped cream. Remember to leave some of the whipped cream for decorations.
6. Pour the orange mixture into the cake dish, over the biscuit base. Refrigerate for about 1 hour, or until the cheese cake is set.
7. Transfer the cheese cake onto a serving dish. Decorate it with orange segments and whipped cream.
8. Serve chilled.

CHILLED STRAWBERRY LOAF

This dessert is rich but absolutely delicious.

Preparation time:
20 minutes plus
3-4 hours chilling time

Serving size:
4-6 portions

1 cup plain yogurt
2 tbsp sugar
½ cup whipped cream
½ cup mixed fruits and nuts (optional)
Loaf mould

1. Dissolve the jelly in hot water and set aside until cool.
2. Add in the yogurt and sugar and mix well.
3. Fold in the whipped cream.
4. Pour the mixture into a wet loaf mould and refrigerate for 2-3 hours until it is set and firm.
5. Dip the mould into lukewarm water for a minute and invert it on a flat dish.
6. Chop the mixed fruits and nuts and scatter them over the strawberry loaf, or decorate as desired.
7. Serve chilled.

Chilled Strawberry Loaf

CHOCOLATE GATEAU

A rich chocolate dessert.

Preparation time:
30 minutes plus
1 hour chilling time

Serving size:
8 portions

CAKE
5 eggs
125 gm sugar
125 gm flour
40 gms cocoa powder
1 tbsp melted butter
8 inch square baking dish

FILLING
2 cups milk
6 tbsp custard powder
1 tbsp cocoa powder

Chocolate Gateau

FOR THE CAKE

1. Beat together the eggs and sugar until the mixture is light and fluffy. Add the butter and light fold in the cocoa and flour.
2. Line the baking dish with some wax paper. Pour the mixture into the dish and bake in a preheated oven for 15-20 minutes.
3. Remove the cake from the dish and cool on a wire rack.

FOR THE FILLING

1. Add the milk into a pan and cook over low heat. Dissolve the custard powder in the milk and stir until the mixture begins to thicken.
2. Add the sugar and the cocoa and mix well. Remove the pan from the heat.
3. When the mixture cools down, add half the whipped cream to the custard.

½ cup sugar

1 cup whipped cream

½ cup sugar syrup (made by mixing 2 tbsp sugar in ½ cup water)

TO SERVE

1. Slice the cake lengthwise into 3 sections.
2. Lay one section of the cake on a flat serving dish. Wet the cake with some sugar syrup. Spread some custard over the cake.
3. Layer another section of the cake on top. Wet it with some sugar syrup and spread some custard over it. Top it with the remaining cake section.
4. Cover the entire cake with the remaining custard, spreading it thickly and evenly.
5. Mix some cocoa powder in the remaining whipped cream and decorate the cake as desired.
6. Keep the cake in the refrigerator for at least 1 hour. Serve chilled.

MANGO MOULD PUDDING

This mango flavoured creamy and nutty mould makes a stunning dessert.

Preparation time:
20 minutes plus
3-4 hours chilling time

Serving size:
4-6 portions

1 cup mango puree
3 tsp gelatine
¼ cup cold water
½ cup sugar
1 tsp cardamom powder
½ cup whipped cream
2 tbsp chopped almonds
2 tbsp chopped pistachios
Your choice of a shaped cooking mould dish

1. Mix the gelatine in the cold water until it dissolves.
2. Add the mango puree, sugar and cardamom powder in a large bowl and mix well.
3. Stir in the gelatine and the whipped cream.
4. Rinse the cooking mould with cold water and pour the mixture into it.
5. Chill in the refrigerator until firmly set.
6. Carefully place the pudding on a serving dish and remove the mould.
7. Sprinkle with the chopped nuts and serve chilled.

JELLY AND CREAM DELIGHT

This dish makes a delicious and satisfying dessert.

Preparation time:
30 minutes plus
2-3 hours chilling time

Serving size:
4-6 portions

1 packet jelly (any flavour)
1 cup thick yogurt
1 cup whipping cream
2 tbsp sugar
2 tbsp candied fruits
2 tbsp cherries
2 tbsp almonds
Ring shaped mould

1. Make the jelly in 1 cup of water according to the directions on the packet, and set aside to cool.
2. Add the yogurt in a bowl and beat well until it is smooth. Gradually pour in the jelly.
3. Carefully place the bowl in ice cold water and continue to stir until the mixture thickens slightly.
4. In a separate bowl, beat together the whipping cream and the sugar. Set aside some cream for decorating. Fold the rest of the cream into the jelly mixture.
5. Chop the candied fruit, cherries and almonds. Keep a little fruit aside for decorations, and mix the rest into the jelly mixture.
6. Pour the mixture into a moistened jelly mould and refrigerate until it is firm.
7. To remove the jelly from the mould, place the mould in a bowl of lukewarm water for a minute. Carefully turn the mould onto a serving dish.
8. Pour the remaining cream in the centre of the mould. Decorate with cherries, almonds and candied fruits. Serve chilled.

CHECKERED COOKIES

Preparation time:
20 minutes

Baking time:
10 minutes

Serving size:
20-25 cookies

FOR THE DOUGH

100 gm butter

100 gm sugar

200 gm flour

1 egg beaten

1 tsp vanilla essence

Food colouring

FOR THE DOUGH

1. Cream the butter and sugar together in a bowl.
2. Add the beaten egg and vanilla essence.
3. Stir in the flour and mix well to form a firm dough.

FOR THE COOKIES

1. Divide the dough into 6 equal portions. Roll out 1 portion into a rectangular sheet about 4 inches x 20 inches.
2. Add different food colours to each of the 5 other portions. Shape each portion into a 10 inch long stick, and stack them all on top of the plain dough sheet.
3. Fold the plain dough around the stack of coloured dough sticks to form a cylinder. Wrap the dough cylinder in cling film and chill in the freezer for about 1 hour.
4. Remove the cling film and slice the dough into thin biscuits.
5. Bake the biscuits in a preheated moderate oven for 8-10 minutes or until done.

COCONUT FINGERS

These mouth watering crisp biscuits are a perfect accompaniment with creamy desserts.

Cooking time:
20 minutes

Serving size:
10–15 pieces

1 tin condensed milk

1 cup grated/desiccated coconut

2 tsp vanilla essence

A few glazed cherries

2 tbsp chopped cashewnuts

1. Mix together the condensed milk, grated coconut and vanilla essence.
2. Spread the mixture over a greased swiss roll tin (about ½ inch deep) and cut into thin long rectangle shapes.
3. Place bits of cherries and cashewnuts on each rectangle.
4. Bake in a moderate hot oven for 10 minutes or until golden brown and firm.

CHOCOLATE ECLAIRS

Preparation time:
40 minutes

Baking time:
15-20 minutes

Serving size:
Makes about 25 eclairs

5 eggs
175 gm flour
100 gm butter
225 ml water
1 tsp vanilla essence
100 gm milk chocolate
2 cups vanilla ice-cream or custard

1. Add the water and butter in a pan and boil for about 2 minutes.
2. Add the flour and keep on stirring till the mixture thickens.
3. Remove the pan from the heat and let the mixture cool slightly.
4. Add the eggs one at a time, beating vigorously. Add the vanilla essence.
5. Transfer the mixture into a large icing bag fitted with star nozzle.
6. Grease a baking tray with butter and then dust it with flour.
7. Pipe the mixture on the baking tray, making 2 inch long strips.
8. Bake in a preheated hot oven for 15-20 minutes or until the eclairs turn golden brown.
9. Remove the eclairs from the oven and allow them to cool on a wire tray.
10. Melt the chocolate and dip one side of each eclair in it.
11. Slice each eclair lengthwise and fill it with ice cream or custard in the middle.
12. Serve chilled.

BANANA CAKE ROLL

This light and moist banana sponge rolled up with cream cheese & nuts is really delicious and can be a tea time treat too.

Preparation time:
40 minutes

Baking time:
12-15 minutes

Serving size:
8 portions

CAKE

100 gm flour

1 tsp baking powder

2 tsp ground cinnamon

3 eggs

1 cup sugar

1 mashed banana

½ tsp lemon juice

1 cup walnuts chopped

1 tbsp powdered sugar

1 large Swiss roll tin (15in × 10 in × 1 in)

FILLING

100 gm cream cheese

50 gm butter

½ tsp vanilla essence

1 cup powdered sugar

FOR THE CAKE

1. Rub the swiss roll tin with butter and generously dust flour over it.
2. Beat the eggs in a large bowl. Gradually add in the sugar. Stir in the mashed banana and lemon juice.
3. Spread the mixture evenly in the swiss roll tin and sprinkle the chopped walnuts on top.
4. Bake the cake in a preheated moderate oven for 12-15 minutes until done.
5. Moisten a hand towel and lay it on a flat surface. Sprinkle the towel with powdered sugar. Loosen the edges of the cake and turn it upside down over the towel.
6. Roll the warm cake and towel together, with the nuts on the outside of the cake. Set aside to cool. The moist towel prevents the cake from sticking together as it cools down.

FOR THE FILLING

1. Mix together the cream cheese, butter, vanilla essence and powdered sugar.

TO SERVE

1. Unroll the cake when it has cooled down.
2. Spread the filling evenly over the cake.
3. Roll up the cake again, this time without the towel, keeping the nuts on the outside of the cake.
4. Place the cake on a serving platter and chill in the refrigerator until ready to serve.

BREAD RASMALAI

Rasmalai is a traditional Indian dessert made from cottage cheese balls and milk. In this recipe I have used white bread instead of the cottage cheese to create an easy alternative for this dish, which is just as tasty as the traditional version.

Cooking time:
30 minutes

Serving size:
6–8 portions

1 lb loaf of white bread
4 cups milk
½ cup sugar
¼ tsp saffron
½ cup oil

For the garnish:
2 tbsp chopped pistachio

1. Slice the bread and cut it into 1 inch squares
2. Heat the oil and fry the bread squares till they turn light brown.
3. Boil the milk for about 10 minutes. Add in the sugar and saffron and boil for a further 5-7 minutes.
4. Soak the fried bread slices in the milk and transfer them on to a serving dish.
5. Garnish with chopped pistachios and chill in the refrigerator for at least 1 hour.
6. Serve chilled.

Bread Rasmalai

CHOCOLATE ALMOND CUPS

This two-in-one truly delicious dessert served in individual glasses tastes every bit as good as it looks.

Preparation time:
30 minutes plus
2 hours chilling time

Serving size:
8 portions

CHOCOLATE MIX

2 tsp gelatine
3 tbsp cold water
4 eggs
½ cup sugar
1 cup whipped cream
1 tbsp raisins
2 tbsp cocoa powder

FOR THE CHOCOLATE MIX

1. In a small bowl, add the gelatine and the cold water. Hold the bowl over boiling water and mix well until the gelatine is dissolved.
2. In a separate bowl, add the eggs and sugar and whisk until the mixture is light and creamy.
3. Add in the gelatine mixture.
4. Slowly fold in the whipped cream, a little at a time, mixing well.
5. Add the cocoa and raisins, and mix thoroughly.
6. Pour the Chocolate Mix into 8 individual dessert glasses and chill for about 1 hour.

FOR THE ALMOND MIX

1. Repeat steps 1 through 4 above.
(Continued next page)

Chocolate Almond Cups

ALMOND MIX

2 tsp gelatine

3 tbsp cold water

2 eggs

½ cup sugar

1 cup whipped cream

1 tbsp almonds (blanched, chopped and roasted)

2-3 drops almond essence

TO DECORATE

½ cup whipped cream

1 tbsp almonds (blanched, chopped and roasted)

8 glazed cherries

grated chocolate

8 dessert glasses

2. Add the almond essence and the roasted almonds.
3. Pour the Almond Mix into the glasses over the chilled Chocolate Mix.
4. Chill for at least 1 more hour.

TO SERVE

1. Decorate with whipped cream, almonds, glazed cherries and grated chocolate.
2. Serve chilled.

PEANUT BUTTER COOKIES

Cooking time:
20 minutes

Serving size:
20–25 cookies

1 cup flour
2 tbsp cornflour
6 tbsp milk powder
½ cup peanut butter
1 cup honey
½ cup raisins

1. Sift together the flour, cornflour and milk powder.
2. In a large bowl, thoroughly mix together the peanut butter, honey and milk, using an electric blender.
3. Add the flour and raisins. Mix well with a wooden spoon to form a soft dough.
4. Divide the dough into 20-25 small balls and arrange them on an ungreased cooking sheet.
5. Bake the dough in a medium hot oven for 10-12 minutes.
6. Cool the cookies on a wire tray and serve at room temperature. Any remaining cookies may be stored in an airtight jar for 2–4 days.

SAFFRON AND PISTACHIO KULFI

Saffron gives this ice-cream dish a beautiful aroma.

Cooking time:
10 minutes

Serving size:
makes 7–8 portions

1 tin condensed milk
1 cup cream
2 tsp gelatine
2 tbsp water
1 tsp cardamom powder
½ cup pistachio nuts (chopped)
½ tsp saffron
2 tbsp warm milk

1. Soak the saffron in warm milk.
2. Heat the condensed milk in a pan. Dissolve the gelatine in water and stir it into the condensed milk.
3. Add the cream, cardamom powder, pistachios and saffron.
4. Transfer the mixture into a freezing tray or individual cups and freeze until firm.
5. Cut into small pieces and serve immediately.

ORANGE KHEER

Kheer is a classic Indian pudding with thickened milk. This version is well worth trying—refreshing orange dessert is a perfect follow up to a hearty main course.

Cooking time:
20 minutes

Serving size:
4 portions

4 cups milk

3 oranges

3 tbsp sugar

1 tbsp chopped pistachios (or grated chocolate)

1 tsp rose water

1. Boil the milk in a pan till it is reduced to 1/3 the original quantity.
2. Add in the sugar and rose water and mix well.
3. Remove the pan from the heat and set it aside to cool.
4. In the mean time, peel the oranges and remove the skin and seeds from each segment.
5. Pour the milk into a glass bowl and arrange the peeled oranges in it.
6. Chill the Orange Kheer mixture.
7. Before serving, sprinkle some chopped pistachios or grated chocolate over the Kheer.

EGGLESS CARROT CAKE

Cooking time:
1½ hours

Serving size:
6-8 portions

- 1 cup flour
- 1 cup sugar
- ¼ cup custard powder
- 1 tsp baking powder
- 1 tsp salt
- ½ cup oil
- 1 cup curd (yogurt)
- ½ cup walnuts (chopped)
- 2 tsp cardamom powder
- 1 cup grated carrots

1. In a large bowl, sift together the flour, custard powder, baking powder and salt.
2. Add the sugar, oil and curd to the sifted flour and beat with a wooden spoon.
3. Add in the chopped walnuts and cardamom powder.
4. Gradually stir in the grated carrots and mix well.
5. Bake the mixture in a preheated moderate hot oven for 1 hour.
6. The Carrot Cake may be served hot or chilled.

STEAMED CURD PUDDING

Steamed Puddings are irresistible—especially when combined with saffron, almonds and pistachios.

Cooking time:
1½ hours

Serving size:
4 portions

3 glass of milk
100 gms curd (yogurt plain)
½ cup condensed milk
2 tbsp sugar
½ tsp cardamom powder
A few strands of saffron
1 tbsp chopped almonds
1 tbsp chopped pistachios

1. Place the milk in a pan and boil it for 15 minutes. Remove the pan from the heat.
2. In a bowl mix together the condensed milk, curd, sugar, cardamom powder and saffron. Add this mixture to the warm milk and pour it into a baking dish.
3. Bake the milk mixture covered in a preheated moderate oven for about 1 hour.
4. Remove the dish from the oven and place it in the refrigerator to chill.
5. Sprinkle the chopped nuts on top before serving.

MASALA COKE FLOAT

Preparation time:
5 minutes

Serving size:
Makes 2 glasses

2 cans of coke
1 tsp lemon juice
1 tsp Chilli Sauce (Pg 49)
½ cup crushed ice
½ tsp black salt
½ tsp cumin powder
2 scoops of vanilla ice-cream

1. Pour the coke into a jug. Add all the ingredients, except the ice-cream, and mix well.
2. Pour the coke mixture into 2 tall glasses, and float a scoop of ice-cream in each glass.
3. Serve immediately.

Masala Coke Float

FRUIT PUNCH

Preparation time:
5 minutes

Serving size:
Makes 2 glasses

1 can pineapple juice
1 packet strawberry jelly
1 banana
500 ml soda water
A few fresh mint leaves
1 cup crushed ice

1. Prepare the jelly according to the instructions on the packet.
2. Add the pineapple juice, jelly and banana in a blender and blend until the mixture is smooth.
3. Pour the mixture into 2 glasses. Add the soda water and crushed ice.
4. Place a few mint leaves on top before serving.

Fruit Punch

LEMON AND ORANGE FIZZ

A refreshing drink that is simple to prepare.

Preparation time:
5 minutes

Serving size:
4-6 portions

500 ml soda water
1 cup fresh orange juice
2 tbsp lemon juice
2 tbsp sugar syrup
A pinch of salt
Crushed ice
1 lemon sliced

1. Add all the ingredients in a jug and stir thoroughly.
2. Pour the drink into glasses and float lemon slices on top.
3. Serve immediately.

ALMOND CHERRY PUDDING

This dish is very easy to make and can be prepared in advance and kept in the refrigerator until required.

Cooking time:
30 minutes

Serveing size:
4-6 portions

1 cup finely chopped toasted almonds

½ cup cherries (tinned)

100 gm cottage cheese (paneer)

100 gm plain yogurt (curd)

½ cup whipped cream

½ cup sugar

½ tsp almond essence

2 tsp gelatine

4 tbsp water

1. Dissolve the gelatine over a double boiler.
2. In a bowl, mix the cream cheese and curd, add the gelatine, sugar, essence, almonds and cherries (keep aside few for decoration).
3. Fold in the cream.
4. Pour the mixture in a dish, cover and keep in the refrigerator till set.
5. Decorate with the remaining cherries.

STRAWBERRY SMOOTHIE

Preparation time:
5 minutes

Serving size:
Makes 2 glasses

1 cup fresh strawberries
1 glass soda (carbonated) water
4 scoops strawberry ice-cream
1 tbsp sugar
½ cup crushed ice

1. Add the ice-cream, sugar, strawberries and crushed ice in a blender and mix well.
2. Pour the mixture into 2 tall glasses.
3. Add the soda water and serve immediately.

COCONUT RING CAKE

Preparation time:
20 minutes

Baking time:
45 minutes

Serving size:
8 portions

225 gm butter
225 gm sugar
225 gm flour
4 eggs
2 tsp baking powder
1 tsp vanilla essence
6 tbsp desiccated coconut
Ring-shaped cake tin

FILLING
100 gm butter
175 gm icing sugar
½ tsp vanilla essence

1. Cream the butter and sugar together in a large bowl until light and fluffy.
2. Add the eggs to the mixture, one at a time, and beat well together. Mix in the vanilla essence.
3. Sift the flour and baking powder together in a separate bowl.
4. Add the sifted flour to the mixture and mix well. Then stir in the coconut.
5. Grease the cake tin with some butter and pour the cake mixture into it.
6. Bake in a moderate oven for about 45 minutes.
7. Remove the cake from the oven and carefully turn it out on a serving platter.

FOR THE FILLING

1. Cream together the butter, the icing sugar and the vanilla essence.
2. Pour the mixture into the centre of the ring cake. Serve warm.

ALPHABETICAL INDEX

□□□